VISIONS OF ORDER

Visions of Order
The Cultural Crisis of Our Time

Richard M. Weaver

Foreword by Russell Kirk
Preface by Ted J. Smith III

**GATEWAY
EDITIONS**

Regnery books may be purchased in bulk at special discounts for sales promotion, corporate gifts, fund-raising, or educational purposes. Special editions can also be created to specifications. For details, contact the Special Sales Department, Regnery, 307 West 36th Street, 11th Floor, New York, NY 10018 or info@skyhorsepublishing.com.

Gateway Editions™ and Regnery® are imprints of Skyhorse Publishing, Inc.®, a Delaware corporation.

Visit our website at www.regnery.com.
Please follow our publisher Tony Lyons on Instagram @tonylyonsisuncertain.

10 9 8 7 6 5 4 3 2 1

Library of Congress Cataloging-in-Publication Data is available on file.

Cover design by John Caruso

Print ISBN: 978-1-68451-549-3
eBook ISBN: 978-1-68451-571-4

Printed in the United States of America

The law of nations is in reality the law of cultures.
—*Charles Malik*

Contents

Foreword

According to Gregory the Great, it has not pleased God to save men through logic. Richard Weaver would have assented to this, knowing as he did the nature of the average sensual man and the limits of pure rationality. Yet with a high logical power, Weaver undertook an intellectual defense of culture, and of order and justice and freedom. This book, published a year after Weaver's death, is the last in a series of three strong, slim volumes: *Ideas Have Consequences*, *The Ethics of Rhetoric*, and *Visions of Order*. They are united by Weaver's appeal to right reason on behalf of the great traditions of humanity.

Dying before his time, at the age of fifty-three, Richard Weaver had lived austerely and seriously all his days. A shy little bulldog of a man from the mountains of North Carolina, as a graduate student at Vanderbilt University he came to know the ideas of the Southern agrarians, by whom he was powerfully influenced ever after. In the College of the University of Chicago he labored for nearly two decades, at odds with the kind of intellectuality prevalent there and nearly everywhere else in modern America.

Among his few close friends in Chicago was the late Bernard Iddings Bell, Episcopalian canon, preacher, and writer. "Richard Weaver distresses me," Canon Bell said to me once, only half in jest; "he grows more like a little gnome every day." Truly it was no congenial climate of opinion in which Weaver found himself enveloped, and he withdrew much of the time to the fastness of his solitary reflections. Yet he never lost himself in pedantry or antiquarianism. Meant to expose and to restrain the illusions of our century, his books and his teaching were instruments for action.

Once Weaver came to visit me at my old house in back-country Michigan. My village of Mecosta was more quiet and old-fangled than his little town of Weaverville, North Carolina, and he was startled at my narrations of rural hardihood and decadence, of a kind he had encountered only in the pages of William Faulkner. Although his life was spent principally in great modern cities, by sentiment and principle he was a champion of the little community, rural life, and immemorial ways. For him the period never arrived when, as he had hoped, he might spend his latter years after the fashion of Henry Ryecroft, writing and meditating in the place where his ancestors had lived and died.

Despite the sympathies which joined us, Weaver and I scarcely were alike in character and temper. Puzzled at my taste for things uncanny, he frowned upon my bohemian relish for the company of pretty girls. No man was less romantic—but none more strongly attached to failing causes. In the cause of humility and peace, he struck manly blows. Vanity he knew not, and he despised the *hybris* of modern times. As he wrote in the essay which is his intellectual autobiography, "Up from Liberalism" (*Modern Age*, winter, 1958–59):

> The intent of the radical to defy all substance, or to press it into forms conceived in his mind alone, is . . . theologically wrong; it is an aggression by the self which outrages a deep-laid order of things. And it has seeped into every department of our life. In the reports of the successful ascent of Mount Everest, the British members of the expedition talked of "conquering" the mountain, but the Nepalese guide who was one of the two to reach the summit spoke of a desire to visit the Buddha who lives at the top. The difference between these two attitudes is a terrible example of the modern western mentality, with its metaphysic of progress through aggression.

Order, the theme of this last book of his, was Weaver's austere passion: the inner order of the soul, the outer order of society.

Deep-laid order has been flouted by the modern sophists, he declared in *Ideas Have Consequences*; ever since the triumph of nominalism, we have been stumbling down the path to Avernus. Perverting the Word, we have disordered rhetoric—and our anarchic rhetoric, in turn, undoes us: so he argued in *The Ethics of Rhetoric*.

Finally, in *Visions of Order*, Weaver assaults the "presentism," scientism, and democratism that are subverting the high old order of our civilization and our human dignity. He did not despair: in a renewed apprehension of the purpose of humane letters, he hoped, we might resist the levelling of culture to a Dead Sea sterility. The mission of Socrates had been Richard Weaver's, too. Thus he concluded his "Up from Liberalism":

> Somehow our education will have to recover the lost vision of the person as a creature of both intellect and will. It will have to bring together into one through its training the thinker and the doer, the dialectician and the rhetorician. Cognition, including the scientific, alone is powerless, and will without cognition is blind and destructive. The work of the future, then, is to overcome the shallow rationalisms and scientificisms of the past two centuries and to work toward the reunion of man into a being who will both know and desire what he knows.

This Platonic view gave purpose and direction to Richard Weaver's life and work. Weaver was surprised at the attention paid to *Ideas Have Consequences*, sixteen years ago; after all, like Isaiah, he was speaking to a Remnant, invisible to him, yet not negligible. This final book, I trust, will speak with courage to as many more men and women who are seeking principles of order. Richard Weaver sowed deep his intellectual seed; and though there are no heirs of his body, the heirs of his mind may be many and stalwart.

Russell Kirk

Preface

On Thanksgiving Day, 1954, Richard Weaver wrote to Richard Cornuelle of the Volker Fund to request support for a proposed new book. After summarizing the arguments of his two earlier works—*Ideas Have Consequences*, published in 1948 by the University of Chicago Press, and *The Ethics of Rhetoric*, published in 1953 by the Henry Regnery Company—Weaver offered this description of the project:

> I now feel that I want to attempt a third book which might, in a sense, complete the other two. It would bring together the problems of order, community, tradition, and expression in some more comprehensive view than either of the others, and I should hope that its analysis might go deeper. It is my feeling that no one has yet adequately exposed the forces of disintegration which threaten so much of modern life. Most social science surveys of the subject impress me

as practically useless because they leave too much out of account and they are too timid. And while I would not presume to do the definitive job, I think that I could push the inquiry a little further.[1]

The ultimate result of this initiative was a slim volume entitled *Visions of Order: The Cultural Crisis of Our Time*. First published by the Louisiana State University Press in March of 1964, more than nine years after it was proposed and eleven months after Weaver's untimely death of heart failure at the age of 53, the book had little immediate impact. It received substantial reviews in only five nationally distributed publications, and of these only two were wholly favorable. Sales began slowly and never really improved. By mid-1974, a full decade after its release, combined sales of the hardback and paperback editions totalled less than 3,000 copies.[2] By 1978, both editions were out of print.

Possible reasons for the book's disappointing performance include ineffective marketing by a press more oriented to academic than popular audiences, less than enthusiastic reviews in conservative publications such as *National Review* and *Modern Age*, and the fact that the book was released at a time when the attention of many potential readers was focused on the dramatic events of the Goldwater presidential campaign. But perhaps the most important reason was the belief, still widespread, that Weaver was working on *Visions of Order* at the time of his death and had left the book unfinished. One prominent source of this belief is Eliseo Vivas, who claimed in his review of the book in *Modern Age* that Weaver "left it in manuscript and had no opportunity to make final revisions."[3]

The truth of the matter is quite different. Weaver's 1954 request to the Volker Fund was rewarded with a $4,500 grant which allowed him to take leave from the University of Chicago and spend the entire 1955–56 academic year working on the book. (It is worth noting that, aside from a single quarter of release time in 1951 to finish *The Ethics of Rhetoric*, this was Weaver's only sabbatical in 29 years of teaching.) Despite a five-month interruption in 1956–57 to see his textbook *Composition* into print, Weaver made steady progress on the project, and in October 1957 he reported to Kenneth Templeton of the Volker Fund that "the book . . . is now virtually completed" and listed chapter titles almost identical to those in the published version.[4] By the end of the following summer the first draft was finished, and Weaver turned his attention to the long and frustrating task of finding a publisher.

The manuscript was sent first to the Henry Regnery Company. But after keeping it "for a very long while—something like a year," they returned it.[5] This prompted "one more revision" of the text, after which Weaver concluded that "it is now in about as final form as I can put it"[6] and resumed the search. In August 1960, on the advice of his old friend Fred Wieck (then director of the University of Michigan Press), he offered it to Farrar, Straus and Cudahy, but with similar results.

At last, in January 1961, an inquiry to the Louisiana State University Press was answered with a warm invitation to submit the manuscript for review. This Weaver did, despite warnings

from a friend that LSU could not provide the professional support he needed, and despite repeated pleas from Henry Regnery
for his company to be allowed to reconsider the manuscript. But
Weaver did not respond to LSU immediately. Instead, he took
more than two months to conduct an exhaustive review of his
work and to solicit criticisms on one of the chapters from a
friend.[7] In the end, however, he decided to change only the proposed subtitle of the book (from the rather forbidding *Essays
toward a Metaphysics of Culture* to *Essays on the Cultural Crisis
of Our Time*). On April 4, 1961, he dispatched the manuscript to
Baton Rouge.

With *Visions of Order* in the hands of an apparently sympathetic publisher, Weaver was able to resume work on two
other major projects, a revised edition of *Composition* and a
new book contrasting the historical cultures of the American
North and South. Neither would be completed before his
death. Meanwhile, at the LSU Press, the first two reviews of
Visions of Order were highly favorable. Weaver was notified
of this in November of 1961 and told that only one more review would be needed. But the third review was negative, and
action on the manuscript was suspended for almost a year.
Only after a change of directors at LSU Press and the receipt
of a fourth (and favorable) review in March 1963 was a decision made to proceed with publication. But Weaver was never
notified of that decision, and he died without learning the fate
of his book.

This brief history suggests at least two important conclusions. First, it is clear that *Visions of Order* was conceived in

1954 and largely written between 1955 and 1957. Further, all of the available evidence indicates that there were no substantial revisions to the manuscript after August of 1960 at the latest. This means that the book is best seen as an expression of Weaver's views in the mid-1950s, not, as is commonly supposed, at the end of his life. This point is crucial to any accurate understanding of the progression of Weaver's thought. In particular, a 1960 letter shows that *Visions of Order* was meant to mark a retreat from the pure Platonism of *The Ethics of Rhetoric* to a more organic view of language and culture and a more explicitly Christian conception of reality.[8] Weaver's writings in the last five years of his life must therefore be seen as products, not precursors, of that change.

Second, it is evident that the manuscript submitted to the LSU Press in 1961 was anything but unfinished. After completing the first draft in 1958, Weaver revised and refined the text repeatedly over the next three years, and on two occasions (in August 1960 and April 1961) he stated explicitly that he had taken the work as far as he could. Thus, whatever one's final opinion of the merits of his arguments might be, those arguments must be seen as the product of long and thoughtful deliberation by an intellect of considerable magnitude and should not be lightly dismissed. This is true even (perhaps especially) in the case of Weaver's iconoclastic attacks on egalitarian democracy, forced racial integration, the cult of the automobile, modern warfare, public education, and the theory of evolution, all of which have been the target of superficial criticisms by those unwilling to address his larger claims.

Weaver's purpose in *Visions of Order* is to show that the restoration of Western culture is both possible and desirable. In order to establish those claims, he constructs a case at two distinct levels of analysis. At the first (and largely dialectical) level, he uses a definition of the essential nature of culture and an analysis of the dominant forces in contemporary American society to show that certain key features of the modernistic worldview lead inexorably to the disintegration of culture. Given this diagnosis, he can then indicate what actions would be needed to effect a recovery. At the deeper (and largely rhetorical) level, he offers an eloquent defense of the idea of culture and a foundational critique of modernism, both grounded in a traditional Western conception of the "nature and proper end of man."

Weaver presents his case in a series of eight freestanding essays, which are formed into a coherent whole by a subtle and elegant pattern of organization. At its most basic level, that pattern divides the series into two groups of four essays each. The first quartet (chapters 1–4) provides a deductive analysis of the nature of culture and the causes of its decline in America and the West. The second quartet (chapters 5–8) rounds out the case by exploring certain themes suggested by the initial analysis. Here Weaver offers contrasting studies of how an overemphasis on status can result in cultural despotism while the subordination of status to function has spawned the barbarities of modern "total war," followed by searching critiques of progressive education ("the greatest single threat to our culture") and those scientific theories that have served to diminish man.

Despite its limited initial success, *Visions of Order* has attracted a large and growing body of admirers over the last three decades, particularly in the academic fields of cultural studies and rhetoric.[9] This should not be surprising. The book includes several of Weaver's best essays (especially "The Image of Culture" and "The Cultural Role of Rhetoric") and its analyses of the nature of culture, the limits of science and technology, and the relationship between rhetoric and dialectic are of profound and lasting significance. In addition, many of the ideas in *Visions of Order* display a kind of heuristic richness which invites their application to other areas of inquiry. For example, the discussion of the problems that arise when a culture attributes "immanence" to its forms is directly relevant to one of the most vexed questions of pluralism: At what point is it permissible for a pluralistic culture to suspend tolerance and act in opposition to a rival culture? In Weaver's terms, tolerance ends, and the defense of pluralism begins, when the rival culture attributes immanence to its forms. Or again, Weaver's discussion of the destructiveness of dialectic in the form of science functions equally well as a foundational critique of ideology, and his analysis of the trial of Socrates may help explain why the adoption by American journalists of a Socratic posture marked by cultural neutrality and systematic skepticism has sparked a massive popular revulsion against the press.

Even granting these qualities, however, it must be acknowledged that much of *Visions of Order* is devoted to a critique of contemporary culture. It is therefore legitimate to question how much relevance a critique of the modernist culture of the mid-1950s can have for the postmodern world of the mid-1990s. After all, the book was written before television's rise to dominance; before the endless procession of movements seeking new and special "rights"; before the "War on Poverty" and the construction of the American welfare state; before the quintupling of violent crime and illegitimacy; before widespread drug use and abortion-on-demand, Vietnam and Watergate, consumerism and environmentalism, affirmative action and political correctness; before the sexual revolution, the information revolution, and the worldwide repudiation of socialism. In a very real sense, *Visions of Order* is the product of a different and more innocent age.

But Weaver took aim at the root of things, and despite the enormous changes in American society and culture over the past generation, there are only two significant instances in which his analysis has been superseded by events. The first of these involves the attempt by social scientists to apply empirical methods to the study of human language and behavior, which was a principal target of *Visions of Order*. This effort collapsed in the late 1970s, due largely to the inability of its proponents to provide satisfactory responses to humanistic criticisms like those that Weaver had advanced. The second instance concerns the determination to "conquer" nature, an attitude of modernism that Weaver reviled as hubristic and impious. However common this attitude might have been in the 1950s, it was quickly suppressed by the triumph of environmentalism in the decades immediately following.

In most other matters, *Visions of Order* stands as a monument to Weaver's prescience. The central focus of the book is the decline of traditional Western culture and its transcendent view of man in the face of relentless attacks by the forces of secular rationalism. That decline has now produced a massive popular reaction and a spreading *Kulturkampf* that is centered squarely on the conflict of worldviews that *Visions of Order* describes. Similarly, Weaver's attacks on the "revolutionary" program of progressive education and his claim that "the world for which the progressivists are conditioning their students is not the world espoused by general society, but by a rather small minority of radical doctrinaires and social faddists" might once have seemed extreme and shrill. But many now endorse such views as an accurate description not only of primary and secondary education, but higher education as well. And in that realm, it is not difficult to see a direct connection between the anti-authoritarian, child-centered practices of progressive education and the emergence of a kind of postmodern "scholarship" in which the search for truth has been supplanted by mere interpretation and the worth of a scholar is determined less by his intellectual achievements than by his membership in some favored group. Nor is it difficult to see, given Weaver's discussion of the organic unity of real cultures, why the effort by the intellectual Left to erect a "multicultural" society on the ruins of forced integration must also end in failure.

In short, for those many now committed to the restoration of American culture, *Visions of Order* can serve as an invaluable guide. Aside from the addition of a preface, this reprinted edition is identical to the original in all respects. The "Foreword" was written in December 1963 by the late Russell Kirk. It is altogether fitting that Dr. Kirk was asked to perform the task. It was on his suggestion that Weaver approached the Volker Fund for support in 1954, and there are many similarities in their views of the plight of Western civilization.[10] It is also fitting that the Intercollegiate Studies Institute should be the publisher of this new edition. Weaver served for many years as a member of the Institute's board and as an associate editor and frequent contributor to its journal, *Modern Age*. It now remains for those who have followed to realize his vision.

Ted J. Smith III
Richmond, Virginia
January 1995

ONE

The Image of Culture

However much opinions of the realities involved may differ, no one can deny that there is widespread discussion of the decline of Western culture. This has been present in philosophical works for more than half a century; the shock of the First World War brought it into more popular organs of discussion, and today one may encounter it, though usually in frivolous forms, in the columns of daily newspapers. That the idea has not merely persisted but has seeped increasingly into the modern consciousness is itself a cultural and social fact of great importance which cannot be overlooked among the signs of the times.

Attempts to dismiss the idea often take the easy route of attributing it to temperamental pessimism or some other condition of the critic. It is alleged that those who say our culture is decaying are those who regularly take an apprehensive view of the future, or they are those who have lost their nerve amid the complexities of an age of transition, or they are those who

1

suffer from nostalgia. The presence of such persons, it is argued, is not peculiar to this age, and hence their warnings are not to be taken as a serious sign that our way of life is deteriorating. The properly constituted man shuns the red-blooded attitude toward things; he goes along with changes because he realizes that change and progress are the law of life and that, although some valued institutions may be disappearing, they will more than be made up for by new ones that are in process of creation. The upholders of this view retort, in brief, that the world instead of growing worse is growing better and that it is really one's civic duty to believe this and to proclaim it.

Thus two largely antithetical views are regularly placed before the public. It is well to see that both of these views are capable of support. One can argue that our culture is in serious decline, and one can argue that it is flourishing and improving. But both arguments cannot be equally valid. Whenever large-scale tendencies are being examined, facts taken from a superficial level and facts taken from a profound one may conflict or point in opposite directions. Like two air masses, one moving at ground level and one moving at a high altitude, they can for awhile pursue opposite courses. If one reads from the top level of phenomena, one may get many signs of assurance which will be contradicted by a look lower down. The real issue in this controversy, then, is one of depth of implication. Yet there can be no implication at all unless one is willing to contemplate an order of human values. The nature and proper end of man are central to any discussion not only of whether a certain culture is weakening, but also of whether such a culture is worth preserving. It is when we look at the depth of implication that we see the real difference between the parties to this argument.

Those who contend that things are going well enough or are improving are found to be nonserious, in the sense of refusing to look at serious things. They glean their data from the novel, or flashy, or transitory sort of development, which often does indicate a sort of vitality, but shows at the same time a lack of direction and a purposelessness. Their data are likely to be the kind that can be quantified in the style of the social scientists or at least of the publicist—so many more people owning record players, so many more books circulating from public libraries, and the like. They ignore the deep sources of tendency which can very easily render nugatory any gains of the above kind. In short, their fact finding is superficial and simplistic, and their claims are made sometimes in a strident tone which is itself a demerit to their case.

Moreover, it is certain that some if not many of the defenders of this optimistic position have a vested interest in "progress," or the present trend of things. A continuation of this trend means for them reputation and money, and they fall in with it as supporters who expect to be rewarded. There are many disintegrative processes which are immediately profitable to those engaged in promoting them, and it is human weakness to covet even such ill-gotten rewards. Therefore it is not hypercritical to look closely at the situation of those who argue for the excellence of modernism to see whether they stand to profit in practical ways from these developments. Not only advertising and journalism but considerable areas of education now invite this kind of scrutiny.

When we turn to the other view, we find that it is made up predominantly of persons who are concerned with the nature of man and the problem of value. They are people with definite ideas of right and wrong, possessing the faculty of taste and consciences which can be offended. Furthermore, they usually will be historically informed, with the result that to them novelty is not always originality nor a fresh departure toward a new horizon. If they are conservative, it is because they have learned the truth of the maxim, "The good is hard," and they know how tempting it is to try to circumvent this. It is my observation that these people suffer a great deal, and their suffering is sometimes used to condemn them, as if failure to achieve complacency were an indictable thing. But it is only those who are capable of discrimination and of feelings *against* things who can be the custodians of culture. Accordingly, I am satisfied that T. S. Eliot made a true appraisal of our times in asserting that "our own period is one of decline; that the standards of culture are lower than they were fifty years ago; and that the evidences of this decline are visible in every department of human activity."[1]

Another way of understanding this conflict of opinion is to recognize that the "optimists" have the current rhetoric on their side even while the "pessimists" have the proof. The modern world has a terrific momentum in the direction in which it is going, and many of the words of our everyday vocabulary are terms implicit with approval of modern tendencies. To describe these tendencies in the language that is used most widely is to endorse them, whereas to oppose them is to bring in words that connote half-forgotten beliefs and carry disturbing resonances. Thus the signs and probabilities are with the optimists, and their task of expression is an easy one, since they have so many ready-made terms at hand. They have the rhetorician's advantage of a language in circulation and a set of "prejudices" in the mind of the majority. It is the object of this writing to bring a rhetoric along with a proof to show that the present course of our culture is not occasion for complacency but for criticism and for possible reconstruction. This requires meeting a rhetoric derived from circumstances with one based more on definition and causal analysis.

I anticipate the further objection that all ages are ages of anxiety just because all ages are in some respect ages of transition. Since transition is a passage to the unknown, a degree of apprehensiveness over what is tentative, unformed, and uncertain is natural. There is some truth in this generalization, yet it would be as absurd to say that every period in the history of a culture is equally healthy and fruitful as to say that every period in the life of an individual is equally happy. It would in fact be intellectual and moral skepticism to deny that some periods are distinct as crises, and the troubled consciousness of modern man gives ample ground for believing that ours is such a period.

The need then is great for a revisionist view of what is known as modernism. The mindless approval of everything modern—indeed, of each dissolution of an old pattern—as something better than what preceded it, or acceptance of the

Spenglerian thesis of inevitable decay, massive and intellectually serious as this is, does not constitute a true dilemma for the
man who wishes to orient himself with reference to the culture
of our time. There is the answer of some third alternative, involving basic principles and leading through free will and effort
to some creative result. The imagination of the time cannot, at
least, leave this possibility unexamined.

One more thing needs to be said about the relation of a
critic to his culture. There is an opinion, by no means easy to
refute, that culture is like a brotherhood: either you are of it or
you are not. If you are of it, you can do something about it to
the extent of carrying it on by living according to its prescrip-
tions. If you are not of it, there is nothing you can do about it,
except perhaps describe it from a distance while missing the
real *Innigkeit*. On this assumption there is no such thing as
aiding a culture from the outside or of aiding it consciously in
any way. If you belong to it, you live in and by it; if you are
outside it, you find the gulf impassable, except to certain superficial contacts. "Culture is culturing," and when a culture
has lost its will to live, outside ministrations are of no use.

But in a further view, there is more than one way of being
outside a culture. One can be outside it simply in the sense of
having been born outside its pale and of having received no
nurture through it. People in this position constitute the kind
of "foreigners" the Greeks called *barbaroi*—"those speaking a
different language." Certainly not to speak the language of a
culture, in the figurative sense, is to suffer effective disbarment.
These persons are alien, even when they belong to another

culture of high development. The man of a different culture has different intellectual and moral bearings, and except in the case of gifted individuals having long periods to assimilate, there is no crossing over, nor any real desire for it. The men of another culture are outsiders, and one expects no more from them than from a friendly stranger, although there is sometimes critical value in an outside view.

There is another type of outsider, however, who may entertain hope of doing something about a culture that is weakening. He is a member of the culture who has to some degree estranged himself from it through study and reflection. He is like the *savant* in society; though in it, he is not wholly of it; he has acquired knowledge and developed habits of thought which enable him to see it in perspective and to gauge it. He has not lost the intuitive understanding which belongs to him as a member, but he has added something to that. A temporary alienation from his culture may be followed by an intense preoccupation with it, but on a more reflective level than that of the typical member. He has become sufficiently aware of what is outside it to see it as a system or an entity. This person may be a kind of doctor of culture; in one way he is crippled by his objectivity, but in another way he is helped to what he must have, a point of view and a consciousness of freedom of movement.

It has been observed, to cite a kind of parallel, that nearly all of the leaders of strong nationalistic movements in the present age were men who had some type of "outside" experience in their rearing or their education. They were men who knew their nations from the inside, but who had also seen them from a vantage point elsewhere. Thus it was with Parnell and Ireland, with Sun Yat-sen and China, with Hitler and Germany, with Gandhi and India. Even Franco is a "Gallego"—not a Spaniard in the true sense. These men had all at one time been far enough removed from their future nations to see what these were, and what they saw engendered in them an urge to define the reality and the consciousness of that nationhood. Although they were "doctors" of nationalism rather than "doctors" of culture, their case shows enough analogy to provide guiding points here. The man who is simply a carrier of his culture may not be armed in the same way to do something about it when it flags. His role may be too much that of simply acting; he can keep in stride, but he cannot coach. For diagnostic and remedial work we may have to turn to those who have in a way mutilated themselves by withdrawal, by a special kind of mental discipline, and by the kind of fixation upon a task which even impedes free cultural participation.[2] We may therefore regard it as no anomaly, but rather as an understandable event, if a person not conspicuously cultured himself should discern what is impairing the health of a culture. Thus it is not the person who has contributed most to a culture who will necessarily have the most useful things to say when the culture shows signs of dissolution.

But what can this person, who is not a paragon of the culture, but who finds himself profoundly stirred by its uneasy situation, actually contribute? From his mixed position he probably can recognize the hostile or disruptive forces. Like the doctor again, he cannot make the object of his attention live, but he can combat those things which would keep it from living. He can point out: this is a disease, this is a poison, this is a bad diet. If the inimical conditions are removed and if there is a true vitality, the sufferer should recover. There are, of course, limits of the analogy of a human culture to an organism, yet culture is a creation in the world, and it must obey certain fundamental conditions of existence.

A radical perspective on the subject may even start with the question of whether culture as such is something we ought to cherish and defend. It would be uncritical to assume that the answer has always been affirmative. Now and in the past, culture in the sense meant here has had to meet open and covert hostility. Certain religions have been largely hostile to it; moralists have condemned it as a frivolity or an indulgence; men of business have been impatient with its demands and its "extravagance"; statesmen of a certain type have opposed it as producing "effeminacy." At present there is a fairly widespread feeling that culture "costs too much" in the sense of gratifying certain educated appetites at considerable expense while the masses are deprived. If the friends of culture were to allow the matter to be put to a popular vote, they might still win, but I do not think that the size of the majority would be reassuring. The public of today does not understand clearly either the nature or the role of culture, and general literacy has not helped the situation.

The claim of culture as such to exist is best explained through its genesis. Man is a special creature in the respect that he has to live with two selves. One of these is his existential part,

his simple animal being, which breathes and moves and nourishes itself. This is man without qualification or adornment, an
organism living in an environment. In this existence he is a very
predictable animal—or would be except that the second self
can have effects upon his somatic appearance and behavior.

The second self is an image which he somehow evolves
from his spirit. It is made up of wishes and hopes, of things
transfigured, of imaginations and value ascriptions. It is a picture to which the subjective part of our being necessarily gives
a great deal, and hence the danger of trying to read it literally
from external facts. A culture expresses itself very extensively
through artistic creation, and, as Suzanne Langer has pointed
out in her *Problems of Art*, we cannot infer artistic vision from
a symptom. That is to say, a mere noting of details without insight and some constructive use of the imagination will not
produce an understanding of a culture.

It appears that even the most primitive people have this
urge to depict themselves in some fashion. Without the pictur-
ization, man feels an unendurable nakedness in the face of his
environment and before the questions of life. From such poverty he rescues himself through projections that include the
natural environment and whatever is suggested by his spirit
regarding the mystery that broods over creation. Look beneath
the surface of the most brilliant cultures of history, and you find
a hunger and a wonderment, reaching even to a kind of mel-
ancholia. Nietzsche has shown how this impelled the Greeks
to create their splendid world of illusion in myth and art.
Impulses of like kind can be found beneath the efflorescence of

Elizabethan England. The more man is impressed with the tragic nature of his lot, the more he dramatizes his relation with the world. A strain of artist in the race causes it to reach out in proportion as its awareness deepens and to throw up great protective creations.

This great yearning of man to *be something* in the imaginative sense, that is, to be something more than he is in the simple existential way or in the reductionist formula of materialism is both universal and proper to him. The latter may be asserted because he is the only creature who asks the question why he is here and who feels thwarted in his self-realization until some kind of answer is produced. This urge to be representative of something higher is an active ingredient of his specific humanity; it has created everything from the necklace of animal teeth with which the primitive adorns his body to the elaborate constructions which the men of high cultures have made to interpret the meaning of life and their mission in it. This is the point at which he departs from the purely utilitarian course and makes of himself a being with significance. It is a refutation of all simplistic histories and psychologies, but it is one of the most verifiable facts about man.

No one has been able to define exactly how a culture integrates and homologizes the ideas and actions of many men over a long period of time any more than how the consciousness gives a thematic continuity to the life of an individual. As far as one can tell, the collective consciousness of the group creates a mode of looking at the world or arrives at some imaginative visual bearing. It "sees" the world metaphorically according to some felt need of the group, and this entails an ordering which denotes dissatisfaction with "things as they are." Of course cultures do respond to differences in what nature has provided, such as the sea, or a kind of terrain, or a hot or cold climate, these having the power to initiate imaginative reactions. But man meets the given part way, and then proceeds with something of his own. So cultures reflect different regions and varying kinds of historical endowment. But the decisive thing is the work of the spirit, which always operates positively by transfiguring and excluding. It is of the essence of culture to feel its own imperative and to believe in the uniqueness of its worth. In doing so, it has to reject others which are "objectively" just as good, yet for it irrelevant. Syncretistic cultures like syncretistic religions have always proved relatively powerless to create and to influence; there is no weight of authentic history behind them. The very concept of eclectic religion and eclectic culture derives from an inappropriate analogy which suggests that a plurality can be greater than one. Culture derives its very desire to continue from its unitariness. Perhaps some deep force which explains our liking for figures of repetition is here involved; we feel confirmed through seeing things repeated in the same way, and departures from the form are viewed as laxity or ignorance.

Evidently this is the reason that every culture in the course of its formation sets up directions from which the members are constrained not to depart. Penalties for violation may be no more than cultural, although sometimes they have been moral and legal. The truth is that if the culture is to assume form and to bring the satisfactions for which cultures are created, it is not culturally feasible for everyone to do everything "any way he wants to." There is at the heart of every culture a center of authority from which there proceed subtle and pervasive pressures upon us to conform and to repel the unlike as disruptive. So culture too is faced with the metaphysical problem of freedom and organization, which rules out the possibility of uncircumscribed liberty. Like all forces which shape and direct, it must insist on a pattern of inclusion and exclusion. This is a necessity of integral being and a fundamental fact to deal with in any plan for its protection.

At this center there lies a "tyrannizing image," which draws everything toward itself. This image is the ideal of its excellence. The forms that it can take and the particular manifestations that it can find are various. In some instances it has been a religious ritual; in others a sacred scripture; in others a literature which everyone is expected to know; codes of conduct (and even of warfare) may be the highest embodied form. But examine them as we will, we find this inward facing toward some high representation. This is the sacred well of the culture from which inspiring waters like magnetic lines of force flow out and hold the various activities in a subservience of acknowledgment. Not to feel this magnetic pull toward identification and assimilation is to be outside the culture.

Such centripetalism is the essence of culture's power to cohere and to endure. There is a center which commands all things, and this center is open to imaginative but not logical discovery. It is a focus of value, a law of relationships, an inspiriting vision.

By its very nature it sets up rankings and orders; to be near it is to be higher; to be far from it in the sense of not feeling its attraction is to be lower. Culture is thus by nature aristocratic, for it is a means of discriminating between what counts for much and what counts for little; this no doubt explains the necessity man feels to create it. It is his protest against the uniformity and dead level of simple succession. He *will* establish a center of value and see to it that the group is oriented toward it. This is his rejection of any merely naturalistic ordering of his life, his declaration of independence from mere environment. Discrimination, selection, and preference with regard to the tyrannizing image are its constitutives.

For this reason it is the very nature of culture to be exclusive. Without the power to reject that which does not understand or acknowledge its center of force, it would disintegrate. We might say that a culture continues by attracting and attracts by continuing. In this way it maintains its identity. There can be no such thing as a "democratic" culture in the sense of one open to everybody at all times on equal terms. To *know* the right thing, without mediating thoughts as to what and when, is to be native born to the culture. An individual absorbs his native culture as he acquires his native tongue, with the most subtle shades of intonation; again, like the idioms of a language, the ways of a culture are rooted too deep in immemorial bias and feeling to be analyzed. If a culture appears arbitrary in the preferences it makes and the lines it draws, this is because it is a willed creation.

The truth most important for us to recognize in our present crisis is this principle of integration and exclusiveness. There is for all things, as Aristotle pointed out, an entelechy, a binding, type-determining factor, which gives to a thing its specific form and property of coherence. The fact that a culture is a spiritual and imaginative creation does not mean that it is any less bound by this pervading law. Just as the skin of a sound fruit protects it from dispersion or evaporation, so the form of a culture keeps it from ceasing to exist through a miscellaneous commingling. Form is intellectual and negative; it sets boundaries which affirm in the very process of denying. The form of a culture is its style, which it asserts against the world of meaningless "democratic" existence. In a highly developed culture this sense of style permeates everything; it is in dress and manners, in art and institutions, in architecture and cookery. It imparts tone to the whole of society by keeping before its members a standard of the right and not right. But this form depends upon the centripetal image of an ideal of perfection and goodness and upon confidence in ruling out what is unlike or fortuitous.

The task in our time of the conservative is to defend this concentration and to expose as erroneous attempts to break down the discriminations of a culture. For once the inward-looking vision and the impulse to resist the alien are lost, disruption must ensue. What was a whole ceases to feel its reason for being a whole, and the different parts may suffer a random distortion—random just because there is no longer a unifying idea to prescribe fitness and size. Parts then get out of line and begin to usurp the places and roles belonging to other parts. This is the chaos that the true friend of culture beholds with deepest apprehension, not only because it deprives him of so

much but because in the masses it can induce monstrous out-
bursts of irrationality. All men, and not merely the sensitive
and the gifted, need the integrating service of this vision, although not all realize that they need it. Lancelot Law Whyte in
his *Next Development in Man* has vividly expressed the power
of this urge:

> Man abhors the absence of integration. He demands
> integration, and will create religions, achieve heroic
> self-sacrifice, pursue mad ambitions, or follow the
> ecstasy of danger rather than live without. If society
> refuses him this satisfaction in constructive form, he
> will seize a destructive principle to which he can de-
> vote himself and will take revenge on the society
> which thought his only demand was pleasure. Vice,
> in this sense, shows the integrating power of virtue,
> of which it is merely the negative form. The
> mass-man readily rejected the utilitarian philosophy
> which had created him and accepted in its place the
> new mass religion of national suicide.[3]

The final sentence, written with reference to the fascist
movements of Europe, reminds us that if no reasonable cultural
unification is offered, an unreasonable one may be invented
and carried to frightful lengths.

The greatest perversion of culture in our time is a misconception of the role of democracy. As the preceding definition
makes clear, a culture integrates a people qualitatively. Under

the widely current misconception, it is supposed that democracy can integrate them as quantitative units—that is, as units without relation to the value structure of the ideal. The most pressing duty of the believer in culture today is to define democracy and keep it within its place, in doing which he not only will preserve it as a viable form but also will protect those other areas of activity which are essential to supply a different land of need.

Democracy is not a pattern for all existence any more than a form of economic activity is a substitute for the whole of living. Truly considered, democracy is nothing more than an ideal of equity among men in their political relationships. Its roots are in the truth that every individual has an inviolable personality, a private experience, and an authentic voice. Every individual is a reporter of what affects him, and he offers motions, as it were, concerning the general political welfare. To make this possible, a democratic state decrees a certain limited equality among its citizens. Even so, this equality is more theoretical than actual. But theories of this kind may have their practical usefulness as well as their noble objects. Thus in a parliamentary assembly we might give each speaker ten minutes to express his views, although we know that one man can say more in ten minutes than another can in an hour. Still, the equality serves the larger purpose. And so with democracy in its consulting of opinions and its counting of votes.

But democracy has to do with citizenship, and as Ortega has pointed out in one of his trenchant essays, our citizenship is the most insipid of our qualities. It concerns the things we have to get done in order to be in position to do things higher in the scale. It is account keeping or household management, an essentially low order of practical activity. It is better to do this well than ill, and it should be done with equity to the individuals involved. But it is senseless to say that dutiful household management is the highest commission of man and that whatever proves instrumental in this must be our principle of ordering all social and cultural life. In our present confusion over the role of culture, this is what is being done with the limited concept "democracy."

When democracy is taken from its proper place and is allowed to fill the entire horizon, it produces an envious hatred not only of all distinction but even of all difference. The ensuing distortion conceals its very purpose, which is to keep natural inequalities from obtruding in the one area where equality has intelligible function. The reason we consent to treat men as equals in this area of activity is that we know they are not equals in other areas. The fanatical democrat insists upon making them equal in all departments, regardless of the type of activity and vocation. It is of course the essence of fanaticism to seize upon some fragment of truth or value and to regard it as the exclusive object of man's striving. So democracy, a valuable but limited political concept, has been elevated by some into a creed as comprehensive as a religion or a philosophy, already at the cost of widespread subversion.

Ortega has wisely pointed out that this is not the spirit of true democracy, but of plebeianism. It exalts the very things that democracy was hopefully inaugurated to combat in the ranks of the people.

The initial result is the wounding of the very sentiment which gave rise to democracy: for the concept of democracy springs from the desire to save the plebs from their low condition. But the doctrinaire democrat, who has converted a technique, democracy, into an end, soon finds himself sympathizing with the plebs precisely because of their plebeianism—their customs, manners, and intellectual tone. An example of this is the socialist creed (for we are dealing here with a creed, a secular religion) which has for one article of faith the dogma that only a proletarian head is fit for true science and reformed morality.[4]

Today we are being asked to accept "democratic living." The eulogistic tone with which this phrase is pronounced invites the question of whether this could be the "tyrannizing image" of some new culture. The answer is "no," if by democracy one means simple communism. Now there are in fact some places where a large measure of equality is in effect among the members without prejudice to the cultural life which they support. Such is true of the communities of some religious orders, where, for example, no outward discrimination is made between those who carry on the work of teaching and those who look after maintenance. It is true also of some educational institutions where the students do a large part of the work; no real distinction is made between those who hold "white collar" jobs and those who labor in the cow barns. Anyone who has visited such a community knows that the social atmosphere there is most agreeable and relaxing. But when one studies the impulse that sustains them, one realizes that the democracy is made possible by a consecration to and a hierarchy of purpose. In the religious communities it is of course the service of the religion; in the schools it is the furtherance of education. Nobody pretends that in these areas all are equal. There is selection according to ability, vocation, and dedication. This structure of purpose and calling is really the insurer of the democracy that exists; equality is maintained where it is useful because there is an overriding aim to be served. If this overriding aim were conceivably withdrawn, it is easy to picture even such communities breaking up into competitive pressure groups among "unequals." It is the authority of the mission which they carry on that keeps inequalities of service in a manageable and pleasing order. Thus the cohesiveness of such communities lies in the idea that informs and possesses them.

What I have here spoken of as true of small associations bears analogy with peoples and nations: a culture is a means of uniting society by making provision for differences. Differences do not create resentment unless the seed of resentment has been otherwise planted. A just man finds satisfaction in the knowledge that society has various roles for various kinds of people and that they in the performance of these roles create a kind of symphony of labor, play, and social life. There arises in fact a distinct pleasure from knowing that society is structured, diversified, balanced, and complex. Blind levelers do not realize that people can enjoy seeing things above them as well as on a plane with them. Societies with differentiation afford pleasure to the moral imagination as an aesthetic design affords rest to the eye. The propaganda of egalitarianism encourages belief that any society embodying distinctions must necessarily be torn with envy and hatred. But theory does not show and empirical observation does not discover that societies having a proper internal differentiation are unhappy. On the contrary, they may be reposeful and content. Of a number of examples which could be used to support this, I choose one described by Goethe in *Poetry and Truth*. Commenting on the Germany in which he had grown up, this great poet and philosopher of life—"Europe's wisest head"—had this to say:

> The tranquillized condition of Germany, of which my native town had formed a part for more than a century, had remained intact in spite of many wars and convulsions. The existence of the most varied social grades, including as they did the highest as well as the lowest, the Emperor as well as the Jew, instead of separating the various members, seemed rather to unite them; and this condition of things was conducive to a feeling of contentment.[5]

Goethe, whose insight told him the true nature of the French Revolution while many of the romantics and rationalists were still befooled, was not deceived by the effect of classes.

> In Germany it had hardly occurred to anyone yet to look with envy on this vast privileged class, or to

grudge its obvious worldly advantages. The middle
classes had quietly devoted themselves to commerce
and the sciences, and by these pursuits, as well as by
the practice of the mechanical arts, had raised themselves to a position of importance which fully com-
pensated their political inferiority; the free or partially
free cities encouraged their activities, so that the members of these classes were able to lead lives of peace and
comfort. The man who increased his wealth or en-
hanced his intellectual influence, especially in matters
of law or state, could always be sure of both respect
and authority. In the Supreme Court of the Empire
and elsewhere, the bench of nobles was faced by one
of the learned lawyers; the freer, less restricted outlook
of the one worked in friendly harmony with the other,
and not a trace of rivalry could be detected between
them in everyday life. The noble felt secure in his exclusive and time-hallowed privileges, and the burgher
felt it beneath his dignity to pretend to their possession by adding a prefix to his name.[6]

This was the Germany of poets, musicians, and philosophers. The classes thrived on a mutual dependence, and the
principle of distinction, far from being felt as invidious, was the
cement that held the whole together. One senses the kind of
satisfaction that was felt in seeing different kinds of people to
the right and left of one and, since it is in the nature of things,
above and below. Not to be overlooked is the fact that a "lowest"

class often finds satisfaction in knowing itself "superior" to other classes in certain respects—in hardihood, in industry, or in religiousness.

A society which is cohesive in this way through classes which have developed naturally out of civic and cultural vocation is in point of fact stronger than one which is undifferentiated. The latter tends to be inflexible and brittle; it does not have the internal give and take of the former. The inner organizations of a structural society act as struts and braces and enable it to withstand a blow which would shatter the other. The whole is sustained by its parts, which afford, as it were, a protection in depth. Nations composed of such societies have proved themselves very tough in international encounters. English society, despite a high degree of classness, has displayed intense patriotism and great power of endurance in crises. The society of the American South, which is formed somewhat upon the English model, has stood up under strong attacks and pressures from the outside through its sense of being organized. All the evidence shows that differentiation which is not fragmentation is a source of strength. But such differentiation is possible only if there is a center toward which the parts look for their meaning and validation. One of the functions of cultural activity is to objectify this center so that it will exist as an ever-present reminder of one's place and one's vocation. A high degree of cultural orientation is, accordingly, a symptom of a healthy society.

In brief, culture is an exclusive, which is to say, self-defining creation, which satisfies needs arising from man's feeling and imagination. Every culture has a kind of ontological basis in social life, and this social life does not express itself in equality, but in a common participation from different levels and through different vocations.

Because of these facts and because of the political contentiousness of our time the question has actually been raised as to whether culture is "reactionary." The question itself reveals a confusion of categories which should never have been permitted. But we know from the words and deeds of Communists and their sympathizers that they make much of this subject and that they are prone to condemn artistic or cultural expression which deviates from their harsh political line. Now it is true, if one takes a very narrow and false view of progress, that much which the world has valued as culture could be condemned as "reactionary." For one thing, the very concept of culture runs counter to blind progressivism, by which I mean that state of mind which cannot measure anything except by number and linear extension. Since culture operates in the realm of quality and offers not greater magnitudes but more refined and intense sentiments, it is an engagement of the spirit lying beyond the thinking of those who have allowed their minds to be dominated by material categories. Speed and mass, virtually the slogans of contemporary Western civilization, are the antithesis of culture. The pointless series of "new developments" and expansions which the modern barbarian delights in look poor and hollow when placed beside authentic creations of the spirit. Since the two impulses move in opposite directions, the one does recede from the other. The barbarian, were he capable of a critical vocabulary, might brand what frustrates his kind of pleasure as "reaction." The possession of culture by historical elites gives some edge to this as a political weapon, but the charge of course mistakes the true gift brought by this creation of the spirit.

Under another aspect culture can be viewed as "reactionary" because it involves a good deal of ceremonial waste, which cannot be explained to those whose vision of life is merely economic and sensate.

This brings up the supremely important matter of style. All culture incorporates the idea of style, which is an homage to an intangible but felt need of the spirit. We hear references to "the modern style" in buildings and other creations where man customarily expresses his desire to impose order and design, yet this seems really to be a negation of style, relieved a little perhaps by imaginative attempts to suggest mass.

True style displays itself in elaboration, rhythm, and distance, which demand activity of the imagination and play of the spirit. Elaboration means going beyond what is useful to produce what is engaging to contemplation. Rhythm is a marking of beginnings and endings. In place of a meaningless continuum, rhythm provides intelligibility and the sense that the material has been handled in a subjective interest. It is human to dislike mere lapse. When one sees things in rhythmical configuration, he feels that they have been brought into the realm of the spirit. Rhythm is thus a way of breaking up nihilistic monotony and of proclaiming that there is a world of value. Distance is what preserves us from the vulgarity of immediacy.

Extension and proportion in space, as in architecture, and extension in time, as in manners and deportment, help to give gratifying form to these creations. All style has in it an element of ritual, which signifies steps which cannot be passed over.

Today these factors of style, which is of the essence of culture, are regarded as if they were mere persiflage. Elaboration is suspected of spending too much on nonutilitarian needs, and the limited ends of engineering efficiency take precedence. Rhythm suffers because one cannot wait for the period to come around. In regard to distance, it is felt that there *should* be nothing between man and what he wants; distance is a kind of prohibition; and the new man sees no sanction in arrangements that stand in the way of immediate gratification. He has not been taught the subtlety to perceive that what one gains by immediate seizure one pays for by more serious losses. Impatience with space and time seems to be driving the modern to an increasing surrender of all ideas of order. Everywhere there is reversion to the plain and the casual, and style itself takes on an obsolescent look, as if it belonged to some era destined never again to appear.

It may be thought negligent that in this exposition I have made no reference to the now extensive studies of various cultures by anthropologists. The reason is that anthropological relativism is the chief quandary to be avoided in the kind of search that is undertaken here. The method of the anthropologists is descriptive, as everyone who has looked at their type of study knows. Essentially geographers and cataloguers of cultures, they are interested in a wide collection of particulars, so that their object could be summed up as *polymathein* rather than *polynoein*: to know much rather than to understand much. I may do some of them less than justice by this charge, yet it is by and large true. What I am certain of is that their practice constitutes a distraction for the one whose interest is in the value of culture and especially of his own culture.

For him the main object is to seize the formal *Innigkeit* of cultural expression and then to decide in what way his own is being menaced or vitiated. Thereafter he is in position to be both doctor and preacher and indeed it is hard to conceive of a man's being thus interested in culture without feeling moved to proceed against its enemies.

I have pointed to the fact that a culture comes into being under the influence of a "tyrannizing" image or vision. I use the word "tyrannizing" hoping that it will be excused its sinister connotations and understood as meaning unifying and compelling. A culture then is a complex of values polarized by an image or idea. It cannot be perfectly tolerant or even tolerant to any large extent because it lives by homogeneity. It therefore has to exclude on grounds which are cultural and not "rational" what does not comport with its driving impulse.

A grave danger arises when this principle is challenged by rationalistic thinkers, as is happening today. In speaking of a culture's power to influence and to bind I have more than once used the word "integrate," since a culture is something unitary gathered about the dominating idea. But "integration" and "segregation" are two sides of the same operation. A culture integrates by segregating its forms of activity and its members from those not belonging. The right to self-segregate then is an indispensable ground of its being. Enough has been said to show that our culture today is faced with very serious threats in the form of rationalistic drives to prohibit in the name of equality cultural segregation. The effect of this would be to break up the natural cultural cohesion and to try to replace it with artificial politically dictated integration. Such "integration" would of course be a failure because where deep inner impulse is lacking cohesiveness for any length of time is impossible. This crisis has been brought to our attention most spectacularly in the attempt to "integrate" culturally distinct elements by court action. It is, however, only the most publicized of the moves; others are taking place in areas not in the spotlight, but all originate in ignorance, if not in a suicidal determination to write an end to the heritage of Western culture.

Two

Status and Function

The preceding chapter has suggested that although every culture is unique in substantive content, it exhibits a certain formal nature which is common to all cultures. This nature reflects basic laws, and when the tendency of a culture to follow these laws is frustrated, either by ignorant popular attitudes or by social derangements, its capacity to offer satisfactions declines. This decline leads to further skepticism regarding its value. If critical thought is to be of use in the reconstructing of a culture, we must isolate the causes that prevent its formal realization.

We have noted the damage that can be done when a political concept breaks loose and spreads lawlessly, imposing its demands in an area where a different principle of ordering is proper. Another serious failure is to be traced to an ontological confusion by which a certain indispensable balance is upset. This is seen today in our failure, both in intellectual outlook and in social regime, to preserve the necessary relationship of

status and function. Modernism is everywhere stressing function at the expense of status, and the more the imbalance grows,
the more precarious and therefore dissatisfied we feel, because
we are surrendering a condition essential to the preservation
of all cultural attitudes and ideas. The reason for saying this
takes us to the nature of things.

Whether we turn either the natural or the introspective eye,
we find objects presenting the two general aspects of status and
function. By "status" we mean the feature of permanence and by
"function" that of change. These properties are the two broadest
headings under which we denote our conception of the world.
Whatever the field we gaze upon, we see things maintaining their
identity while changing. Things both *are* and *are becoming*. They
are because the idea or general configuration of them persists;
and they are becoming because with the flowing of time, they
inevitably slough off old substance and take on new. The paradox
of both being and becoming is thus continuously enacted. We
say that there is a "nature of things," but this nature ever appears
in a changing embodiment, so that if we attended only to the
latter, we should no sooner say of a thing that "it is" than we
should be obliged to say "it was" or "it is now something else." It
is an ancient observation that "no man steps in the same river
twice," yet we continue to conceive it as a river and to call it by
one name. At one and the same moment permanence holds us
enchanted and change urges us on.

The oak tree in the forest is none the less an oak tree though
it passes, in a century and a quarter, from a tiny shoot to the
sturdy giant of seventy feet. Through all its seasonal dormancy

and growth, its interchange with water and air, it remains an oak tree, a fixed kind in nature. It possesses status in a world of change. The physicist's account of the whorl of molecules that make it up will not cause us to refer to it as anything but "that oak tree."

We look upon the individual person and see him maintaining his persona all the while he passes through the seven stages of life. Despite changes, he is the same: one man legally identifiable under one name, through all his natural and mental processes of assimilation and elimination. He grows in size, alters in appearance, and he may even change somewhat in personality, but the thread of his selfhood persists and he never undergoes amalgamation with the circumambient world. Our dealings with him are conditional upon our understanding that from year to year he is one individual, preserving a self amid the flow of materiality.

So it is with art styles. We have a Greek art, a Byzantine art, an art of the Italian Renaissance. They have their developments and periods, their identifiable creations of individual artists, yet they remain an art form, with typical features of perspective and emphasis. This is their character, their formative principle, which allows us to discriminate them. The individual works participate in a common idea.

The same process is visible even when we look at the political state. It persists under one name, and it may even affirm in its organic law that it is indestructible. But its old leaders pass on or are removed, and new ones appear. After a twenty-year absence, one would come back and find the leaders looking

different in almost any country. But while these individual par-
ticles are being shuffled and replaced, "the state" goes on, maintaining some character and identity through all the changes.
The most conservative state must yield something to the pressure of historical increment, and the most "progressive" one
conserves something that it considers its special form and
spirit.

This duality of permanence and change is the universal appearance of existing things, and it seems to express an ineluc-
table condition of fulfillment. It is an original provision, ubiq-
uitous and profound, which we are compelled to respect even
in maintaining our human creations. To see how they are mani-
fested in cultures, we need to study each more closely.

The status of a thing is its attained nature and quality or its
possession of being. It is repugnant to mind as well as to feeling
to think of the world as pure becoming or as something which
never is because it is forever in process. We feel intuitively that
things have a being, that they show a certain definable essence
which we can grasp through the intellect. The world may be constantly flowing, yet it is a world. The very idea of existence is
frustrated if we imagine only a continuous stream or if we think
of a thing as surrendering itself before a self can ever be established. We could never become attached to something that never
is. If reality were merely a flux, "selves" and "natures" would be
illusions, and we could never consciously deal with the world.
Both theory and observation prove that there are perdurances.
Our existence is such that we alternate between expectation and
fulfillment, and without fulfillment, expectation would cease.

Therefore status, or the achieved state of things, is ontologically a necessary ground for our activity. It is one half of this lawful dichotomy of existence.

It is this half which today needs the attention of the critical mind. But to avoid appearance of neglecting the other, let us first acknowledge that the world in which man is born to seek out his salvation is in part a world of historical process. Religious, philosophical, and literary studies of man concur in teaching that he is born to a condition of "action and liability" where he must work out the "awful experiment of time." The continual becoming of things forever confronts us with challenge, testing our quality and our sense of direction. Even while man has status, he is under the absolute necessity of functioning, as each sequent heartbeat makes plain. He is actor and creator, and indeed the mere conservation of status calls for action. The functioning of man is in his adaptation to change, his dealing with the incessant transiency of things in such a way that some line of meaning in his conduct is preserved. Function is the role of *homo faber*, or as this could be translated into a modern equivalent, "man the engineer."

The particular urgency with which this essay deals is an unbalancing in which man represents himself too exclusively as engineer and supposes that the finding of means to practical ends should be the whole of existence. For today function increasingly displaces status, and people can be found to say that there is no value in status or that status only clogs activity. These people are often self-styled proponents of culture and they may even give a large amount of time and energy to what they conceive to be cultural activities. But because they are mistaken in principle, there is small hope of saving such culture as we have inherited unless they can be awakened or somehow checked by others. They are the "functionalists," and they bring us to the threshold of this cultural crisis.

It will be found that every culture which creates rewarding social structures and works of the imagination has its existence through an equipoise of function and status. This is a condition of equilibrium, a delicate balancing of opposites for which, on the lower levels, there are analogies in the ways in which an organic body maintains an equilibrium of matter. In its healthy state it takes in enough to sustain and to offset; it preserves a balance. A living body must have salt, but too much salt would act as a fatal poison. On its own level of existence, culture accommodates things likewise; it utilizes things which in unmeasured quantities would prove deadly. These are the terms in which we have to think of such antithetical components as status and function. These can be destructive to each other, if either gets beyond measure, but held in the right proportion, they sustain the cultural body. Too much status will obstruct function, and too much function will disrupt and destroy status. Yet these hostile principles meet to advantage, and the task of the prescriptionists of our culture is to discern what changes are necessary to get them back into a proper relation. It is just this coming to terms with the round of life, this domestication of the whole range of needs that puts man in position to express and satisfy himself with cultural creations.

Many cultures of the past have come to suffer from an excess of status which leads to petrifaction. They have done this through too much reliance upon forms and styles as achieved and as not needing the alert attention that is required for a living continuance. Status has to prove continually that it has meaning to avoid over formalization. It is thus not excused from responsibility. It has to meet new conditions, to absorb into itself something of changed conditions while maintaining that identity which is its stuff. This necessity can be illustrated in the following way. We are at liberty to think of a title in itself as an empty thing, a mere cipher. Like ciphers, no number of titles can really dignify where active worth is absent. But if the cipher is placed after a digit, it has the power of multiplying that by ten. So in a manner with status. If it is in conjunction with genuine worth, ability, or achievement, it tends to raise these. It changes the man's representation in his own eyes and in that of others; it lifts him and braces him for still greater achievement. Title is a sign of status; when it combines with function, it produces a value which either alone is incapable of producing. The reference here is not to titles of nobility, although in real aristocracies these have served in the same way. The very fact that in the traditional societies of the West we retain civil and professional titles shows a continuing sense that they have some positive value as indicators of achieved status. Those sans-culottes and egalitarians who are incensed by the very idea of titles and badges, insisting that everyone be merely "Mister" or "Comrade" or "Joe," are failing to see one of the chief incentives to self-direction and self-discipline. This is the very human desire to have one's achievement recognized, classified, and represented to the world.

Those aristocracies of the past, whether bearing titles or merely surrounded by some deference to status, justified their role by both being and doing. They enjoyed status, but when emergencies arose, they took the field and showed that they were not afraid to meet a test. Most importantly of all, their recognized status provided a kind of sanctuary from which they could defy public opinion when they thought that opinion wrong, and the willingness to do this is essential to the idea of leadership. Men like George Washington and most of the other leaders of the American Revolution were not afraid to step into perilous circumstances. They risked their extensive property holdings and they acted counter to a strong and perhaps majority opinion in conducting a revolutionary movement. Washington is our finest example of the type which combines consciousness of status with capacity for action. He was a patrician and an heir to status. Yet we see him surveying the western wilderness at sixteen, fighting with Braddock against the French and Indians, and finally leading American arms to success in a seven-year struggle against Britain. We may assume that Washington in his latter years felt no embarrassment over being addressed as "Your Excellency." He had elevated himself through character and action. This type of role, with its subsequent self-representation, gave this nation the purest and ablest group of patriots it has ever known.

To be contrasted with this is the kind of aristocracy which does not keep itself alive by function. In his discussion of the social condition of France in the years before the French Revolution, de Tocqueville emphasizes the fact that the French nobility had degenerated from an aristocracy into a caste. The truth of this appeared in two circumstances: the nobility no longer performed any type of service, and it was isolated from the communal life of the nation. Thus it was functionless and it was out of organic relationship with the society which supported it. This nobility possessed only status, and therefore its days were numbered. Caste may well serve as a name for a condition of mere status, a condition in which half of existence is given up in blind engrossment with the other half. Thus caste is always an evidence of imbalance and a sign that the human situation has been misconceived somewhere along the line of development. De Tocqueville goes on to contrast with this the British nobility, which, for all its selfishness, maintained a role of leadership and service. That it survived the French nobility and kept the respect of the world into present times proves that its combination of status and function preserved it as a part of organic society and of a viable culture.

These are some of the dangers of status. But the society which tries to put forward function as the sole criterion runs equally grave dangers, and these are the dangers we are faced with today.

To understand the defect of a society which tries to insist upon function as the single standard of measure, we must note that it seeks to base itself upon instrumentalism. There is no way, however, in which instrumentalism can provide an ideological basis for society. Its one test for any individual or any institution is success, but we cannot judge how well a thing works in the absence of goals of working. Activity is not the judge of its own appropriateness and achievement. There must always be something against which the activity is measured, and this can be provided only by intuition and philosophical reasoning. Basically, the failure of the purely functional society lies in its unwillingness to ask, "What is man?" Unless man has some definite idea of what he ought to be, no amount of activity can serve him for the simple reason that the activity cannot be organized. Just as it is logically impossible to have practice without theory, so it is impossible to have social and cultural activity in the meaningful sense without some idea of a valued state of being. The functionalist refuses to bring consciousness and mind to bear upon the state of things because these imply criteria that direct function, encouraging it here but checking it there. This is a position which recognizes the independency of thought.

A purely functionalist or activist society is likely to pride itself upon judging people solely by "what they can do." This seems appealing, and it is true that no man should be exempt throughout life from some real testing of his capacity for function. But function is simply too partial to serve as the sole criterion, and it probably never would have gained such acceptance as it has now if our times had not done so much to discourage reflective thinking. Even so, it does not require a great deal of reflection to discover as a starting point that there are two categories of persons who cannot be judged simply by "what they can do": these are children and the elderly. Neither can justify themselves in competition with people who are in their prime, and therefore they have to be protected by acknowledgment of their *status* as human beings. You cannot kill a child because he is weaker than you, and you cannot turn an elderly person out to starve because he is no longer capable physically or mentally of the work expected of a vigorous adult. Both have rights which do not depend upon a purely instrumental view of their natures. Society in general has admitted this without even raising the question, which is evidence that the principle is basic. But modern society in its practice is doing many things which obscure or weaken the principle of status.

One of the most obvious of the imbalances thus created is the modern deification of youth. The whole trend of our commercial, political, and social world is toward giving youth the primacy. The rhetoric of advertising, the cult of political "liberalism," and the preference of activity over contemplation are manifest products of this trend. By youth I mean of course those who are in the health and strength of young manhood and womanhood—let us say eighteen to thirty-five. Now this virile group has its status too and its special virtues, but it is not the thoughtful part of mankind. Its physical senses are at their most acute, but it has not acquired the wisdom which comes from watching this passing show for several decades. It is characterized by exuberance, appetite, keen passions, and sanguinity. It has not had time to generalize its experiences and to learn that the panaceas of the hour are often very ancient things in some newly got up dress. But if we do judge people by "what they can do" and understand by "doing" the kind of outward and physical thing which is most easily measured, this group will inevitably get too large a share of attention.

In summation, the greatest weakness of a function-oriented culture is that it sets little or no store by the kind of achievement which is comparatively timeless—the formation of character, the perfection of style, the attainment of distinction in intellect and imagination. These require for their appreciation something other than keen senses; they require an effort of the mind and the spirit to grasp timeless values, to perceive the presence of things that extend through a temporal span. Mere speed of reflexes and quickness of vision are not the prime necessities for this kind of appreciation. A society which tends to hand its leadership over to those who perform best on the functional scale inclines naturally to make physical measure a more decisive factor than it ought. This is an emphasis that discourages intellectual attainments in the culture.[1]

It will be instructive to turn to a historical example of these two cultural imbalances we have described. We have had in the United States during the latter half of our history convincing illustrations of what happens when this principle of equilibrium is ignored. The North-South polarity of our American culture must be understood in these terms. North and South have consistently opposed one another; each has charged the other with unreasonableness and perversity in its attitudes and institutions. Moreover, each is puzzled and indignant over what it regards as the groundlessness of the other's charges. This opposition can be referred to the cause we are now considering.

The South has attached too much weight to status. The North, or in general that part of the country to which the sobriquet "Yankee" is applied, has attached too much importance to function.

From early times the Southerner enjoyed a condition of life which gave him an awareness of status. The owner of lands and the inheritor of the medieval idea of station felt conscious of rank. For a considerable period he was somebody in the functional sense, as is shown by his part in our Revolution and in the expansion of the nation down through the presidency of James K. Polk. Even in highly aristocratic Charleston, there were men who took pride in being self-made and who urged the value of practical experience as a part of education.[2] At some point, however, status seems to have passed beyond the line of equilibrium. It began to be thought of as something sufficient in itself. To be born into the owning class was supposed to confer all that one needed. Social status came almost to play the part of royal blood in other societies, and out of this there developed a dangerous kind of presumption, blinding to those who held it and irritating to most who encountered it.

This disposition to rely upon what one was supposed to be, rather than upon what one could be effectively, had undeniably a weakening influence upon Southern manhood of this class. This truth became evident following the Civil War, when many Southern men turned over the struggle even to make a living to their more valiant mates and lived idle and pointless lives, while the political power they had once wielded was seized by the poor white leaders and the demagogues. The loss of initiative following enemy domination had much to do with the fact, but the truth remains that a more rigorous land of ideal might have enabled them to fashion more than they did out of the prevailing chaos.

There is, of course, another side to this picture, for belief in status contributed a great deal that was admirable in Southern society. It contributed the valuable element of stability, without which happiness is but doubtfully secured. It contributed much to the freedom and independence of the individual, because the man who "knows where he stands" is always more confident in approaching others and in declaring his opinions than the man who neither knows who he is nor where he is from. It kept the individual from being intimidated by public opinion. Like the judge portrayed in Robert Penn Warren's *All the King's Men* (which is unerring in its knowledge of Southern psychologies), this type of man did not care what people thought about him, for "he knew that he was a great man." This attitude can issue in an insufferable conceit, but this should not be allowed to blind us to the element of noble self-confidence which is its proper origin. Finally, it imparted a spirit to society which rebuked slothfulness of manner and thought and encouraged emulation. Carl Bridenbaugh, not a particularly sympathetic student of Southern society, has remarked that "the very fact of status, accepted as a yard-stick, regulated their [the Southerners'] behavior and gave it tone."[3] The fact that Southern culture has reminded European visitors of European culture more than any other in the United States seems definitely related to this belief in status. More than any other section, the South tended to be a culture of *estates*. In this way it was a conservative order, in some degree comparable to the European establishment.

But if the South put too much weight on this side to maintain the proper balance, its great opponent the North put too much on the other.

Northern society has been described by those who admire it as dynamic and by those inclined to question it as restless and overly aggressive. Both descriptions suggest that its lack of equilibrium comes from an overemphasis of function. Much of the criticism leveled at this section concerns the dominance of the businessman type. The North has in general taken the view that it is the duty of man to carry on an unceasing work of exploitation, which is variously denominated "business," "development," and "progress." It may be recalled here that Calvin Coolidge, that narrowest and least imaginative of all American Presidents, who was in many ways representative of this outlook, once declared from the White House that "the business of America is business." The winning of the West was largely a northern enterprise, and the industrialization of the country was almost exclusively such. Almost everything in the North, including social alignments, has been geared to an expanding business "civilization." The stories of young men who started out with only their bare hands and became immensely wealthy have been the most approved American sagas. There occurred, consequently, an extraordinary adulation of function or capacity to show results, and with it the creation of a class of "functionalists" called "businessmen." A few years ago Professor Elijah Jordan pointed out in his original book entitled *Business*

Be Damned that never before in history had this type of person
formed a class enjoying social prestige. There have always been
activists and gain-getters, but it was reserved for the modern
age, under American leadership, to give the successful
gain-getter an honorific in the form of "businessman." Professor
Jordan has characterized the mentality of this new class, whose
status is all function, in these terms:

> In business intelligent and serious interpretation of
> facts is never called for; intelligence is not involved
> at all. Only the individual with the strongest motives,
> motives least checked by moral sensitiveness, can
> survive. The psychological make-up of the business
> "mind" is therefore a mere collection of disconnected
> motives, impulses entirely without conscious direc-
> tion or moral unity of purpose, hence without intel-
> ligence. A "decision" of such a mind is merely the
> triumph of one motive, the worst, over the rest, par-
> ticularly over any impulse to sympathetic apprecia-
> tion of another's stake in the situation. The latter
> impulse is "inefficiency."[4]

The description is bitter, but the author states an essential
truth. If it is taken as a picture of the mind which develops
when all the virtues are subordinated to successful gain-getting,
it is historically authentic. For a long period, industrial and
plutocratic society elevated this narrow and undeveloped type
of mind to positions of social and intellectual leadership.

Indeed, it has often been mentioned that the Civil War, which secured for the North hegemony over the Union, put an end to the leadership of the minister and the lawyer, whose status involved some degree of cultural attainment, and replaced it with that of the business entrepreneur.

It is true that men of this class in many instances tried to atone for their partialness by lavishly endowing universities, art galleries, museums, and other such institutions for the propagation of culture. But these things are externals. They are useful vehicles and receptacles, but in themselves they cannot engender the spirit which creates culture. Meanwhile, the adulation of function does constant damage to that spirit. It cultivates a mood of aggressiveness which is unwilling to let anything be, perhaps out of a subconscious fear of its enemy, status. It inaugurates the infinite series of progress, which is fatal to stability. It is hostile to the mood of contemplation, which nourishes both the aesthetic and the religious life. Finally, it accompanies all of these things with material distractions which only the most self-directed can overcome. Those Americans who went to Europe in great numbers during the final quarter of the last century and the first quarter of this one, and whose exodus has often been satirized, were fleeing from a very real danger. They were fleeing a society so dedicated to function that it left little opportunity for those quieter moments which a man must have to create or to ponder what living is for. A disequilibrium had been set up and institutionalized. It was called the life of progress and success.

That the North attached excessive importance to function and the South to status is a basic diagnosis of American culture. It was a cultural tragedy that after the Civil War the two sides hardened in their attitudes. Border states like Maryland and Kentucky have given a taste, if only a taste, of what an attractive and genial culture could spring up on American soil when the two conditions of status and function are kept in relative balance. If this had prevailed generally and if there had been a development of the theoretic and literary sides, the United States as a whole might have produced a culture of the first rank by now. But the majority of the nation succumbed to the imbalance of function, and if this discussion is to be more than academic, we must examine the possible means of getting back to an equilibrium.

This directs our inquiry to the ultimate source of status, the offsetting concept to the incessant change of the world.

The idea of status is created by the mythopoeic consciousness of man; and in the decay of myth, which has been recognized by many social critics as a major feature of modernity, one can identify the forces that are working against status.

Myths are great symbolic structures which hold together the imaginations of a people and provide bases of harmonious thought and action. They posit a supersensible world of meaning and value from which the least member of a culture can borrow something to dignify and give coherence to his life. Obviously the myth is not born of calculation, nor can its "function" ever be measured. As Ernst Cassirer points out, myth defies the analytic process which is used with empirical data.

Most important of all, mythical time has no definite structure; it is always "eternal time." From the point of view of the mythical consciousness, then, the past has never passed away; it is always here and now. Therefore myth is the greatest of all conservators of the significance of things against forces which would make significance contingent upon a present, topical urgency. Whatever has become myth has acquired a status invulnerable to two things: the positive point by point correspondence of empirical testing, and the likewise empirical testing of present function.

The mythopoeic faculty of man, like his ability to create symbols, is a distinctively human attribute, and its exercise is a satisfying of one of his deepest psychic hungers. Man creates myths because he feels that, in the language of Goethe, "all before us that is passing sign and symbol is alone." His myths are the distillation of this meaning, a humanized quintessence of the great pageant. In myth, which is timeless, which expresses some idea of value, and which cannot be dealt with or destroyed by the method of analysis, man expresses a reality which is subjective but which is nevertheless part of the totality. It is his highest response to the insistent question of his own significance. Thus the truth of myth, like the quality of status, is something that must be seized intuitively. Either it is seen in its persuasiveness as one of humanity's archetypal ideas or it is not grasped at all.

All idea of status, it can now be said, depends on the presence of this overriding mythic consciousness. For cultures always attach value to what they wish to attach value to. If this seems meaningless, we must remember that there are ways of

"demonstrating" that some attachments are "unreasonable."
That is to say, one can step outside the lines of desire and say
that this or that thing would be a better object of desire than
the particular one in question. But this is like saying that men
ought to value a quantity of iron above a quantity of gold, which
leaves out of account the fact that affinity goes where it will in
obedience to some paralogic of value. In similar fashion culture has its own ways of valuing status, which is not always
apart from function, but is never a simple exponent of it. This
does not mean that it is completely irresponsible, as I propose
to show in the chapter on "Forms and Social Cruelty." Our
subjective world is part of the whole world and is linked up
with the remainder of the totality. This imposes certain obligations which preclude a pure autonomy. The point here is that
a merely ponderable measurement always endangers status,
and there is ground for saying, by way of a general observation,
that an individual's position in society is higher in proportion
to his belief in imponderables.

Now the creation and preservation of myth itself are linked
up with an acceptance of the poetic nature of all language.
Language is poetry in a valid sense because it isolates and defines
out of the variety of our perceptions the things that have human
importance. It is the essence of the mystery of naming that to
name a thing is somehow to domesticate it and to give it a place
and a rank in our humanized world. But to do this with belief in
what we are doing calls for a confidence in language which some
contemporary theorists are seeking to undermine.

In the past few years there has developed a great self-consciousness about language, which seems to proceed from a feeling of discomfort in the presence of it. The feeling itself comes in turn from a notion that man is a prisoner of language. This has prompted students imbued with the scientific temper to try to put language through the same mill that is used to reduce other things to scientific manipulatability. Their work takes the form of studying language from the outside and drawing up a behavioral report. The process actually fractionates language by breaking it down into its ultimate physical constituents, whereafter the recurrence of these is tabulated and correlated. Normative and prescriptive ideas are rigidly excluded, with the result that there is no explanation of why the elements of language leap together into meaningful configurations. The *Gestalten* of language thus become as irrelevant as the compulsive figurations of the myth.

This has an important effect upon the idea of status for the reason that language, once created, is a great indicator and conservator of value. The names of things for one generation are by and large the names of things of the next generation and those following. Names themselves do not share, except to a slight extent, in physical evolution. We know this has induced some to declare that language therefore falsifies or that it imprisons the dynamic world in a fixity which is an illusion. For these people language becomes a source of error the moment it imposes the stasis which all names carry upon the phenomena of the world. The extreme of this theory would make impossible language in the conventional sense; there would be in its stead something registering and transmitting like a photo-electric cell.

It is clear that this theory stands in the way of axiological realism. It offers no account of how language can give insight into the enduring values of things. If language is sometimes partial in its description of referents, it is also additive in the respect that it contributes to our perception of their value. There is no basis for insisting that it be a physical replica of the thing symbolized, but there is basis for insisting that it be expressive of our "imagination" of the thing, which will carry some element of feeling. The theoretical aim of the functionalist is to make language special for every situation; the desire of the traditionalist is to have it carry a tradition of meaning which makes the thing named intelligible in the framework of the culture.

This case needs to be urged because words are the designations of status. Any view which reduces them to mere exponents of special situations takes away the power they have as a specifically human means of expression to confer something that has its origin in the imagination. For words are relative to thoughts, not to things; it is impossible to show that a word has the same kind of connection with the thing it is standing for that it has with the mind of the user. In fact it is impossible to show at all that a word has connection with the thing for which it stands. The only connection that can be demonstrated is with other words in the vocabulary, and this must be done through a poetical operation. Language is peculiarly intimate with mythopoeic value, and scientistic attempts to view it as only a part of behavior would deprive it of its capacity to serve the myth. An axiological view of language is, therefore, necessary to recover the source of status.

The very fact that language has a metaphorical function, and indeed, metaphorical origin, is a further illustration of the necessity. For the perception of likeness is essentially an imaginative enterprise, and the likeness that is perceived is a first step toward generalization. To say that something is like something else is to affirm a certain basis of continuity. The conservatizing and stabilizing function of language is thus being utilized whenever we make the transference of meaning which is embodied in a metaphor. The tendency of metaphor is plainly toward a unity of conception whereas that of simple denotation is toward diversity. In order to have meaningful status we must have something ascending up toward an ultimate source of good. Otherwise status is random and singular, and the various statuses which a society recognizes would not be capable of offering resistance in depth to whatever would collapse them. Consequently culture's "mythic cover" and its power to create status are aspects of the same feature.

The decline of myth in modern societies and the ensuing decay of status are related also to the disappearance of "place." This is a truth at once obvious in its occurrence and difficult for analysis. It must be evident to all, however, that certain facts of technological development have worked to diminish the separateness of places. Modern man has acquired an excessive mobility, so that it means nothing, as compared with yesterday, for him to be in one place or to go to another. The automobile and the airplane whirl him about with such velocity that it now has little significance to be in or from a place: one's situation can soon be altered. In the book of modern progress this is, it hardly needs saying, listed as a credit, yet there is much to make us feel that it is a debit when all things are considered. There is something protective about "place"; it means isolation, privacy, and finally identity. We cannot rationally wish to be nowhere or everywhere at once. To be somewhere is necessary to our standing—to our status.

For essentially the same reason, this terrible mobility is fatal to mythical constructs. Myths have always developed among a people occupying one region for a long period of time and developing a strong provincial consciousness. The heroes and demigods of these great creations are always dwellers somewhere (as the gods of Greece on Olympus), and the idea of a cosmopolitan mobility and interchangeability is foreign to them. To take away place is to take away the locus of myth. I am convinced that nothing has done as much to weaken the myth-making faculty of man as this modern pressure against the idea of place, expressing itself even overtly in a desire to "annihilate" space.

It may indeed seem the height of futile protest to argue against anything as highly prized by modern man as his mobility. But this is not the place to be gingerly practical; the purpose of this writing is to isolate the real causes of modern disintegration and to see whether the effort that would be required to halt it is within our civilization's capacity for renewal.

To summarize the situation: the hope of bringing status back into the intellectual and moral life of our time depends upon an expansion of consciousness. We must admit again to full standing the kind of knowledge that mythical representation embodies. This calls for giving up the false notion that we can find the meaning of life by searching out the composition of the material world. (Of course when a trend becomes as powerful as this none of us are likely to avoid being trapped into some of its false position.) The modernistic searcher after meaning may be likened to a man furiously beating the earth and imagining that the finer he pulverizes it, the nearer he will get to the riddle of existence. But no synthesizing truths lie in that direction. It is in the opposite direction that the path must be followed, toward those broad, speculative, coherent, and heuristic ideas which tell us indeed nothing of the structure of the atom, but cause us to see that these images, feelings, events, intuitions, and dreams which fill our lives have some meaning beyond their mere presence. This will be knowledge of transcendental ideas, and it will bring with it the now largely lost conviction that man *is* somebody.

Then we must again become sensitive enough to realize that "place" means privacy and dignity, and that it is against the interests of our highest feelings to destroy the idea of station.

Man is not created to live without space or place any more than he is designed to stand on the point of a needle, and the confusion of categories which permitted this notion to arise is one of the problems for the student of intellectual culture. The recovery of the principle of status involves a series of retrievals. The river of knowledge must sometimes turn back on itself; now it needs to return to show us that myth and language are joint sources of expressing and conserving value, and that the value of a place to stand, which was hardly questioned until the present, has its analogical expression in the world of cultural consciousness.

THREE

The Attack upon Memory

Between myth and status and memory there is a necessary connection. Clearly people cannot identify or appreciate status unless they can carry with them a memory of society's hierarchic structure and of the image in response to which it has framed itself. If men were to view one another as created anew each day, they would see themselves in original, not achieved or conferred relations. Every individual's desire is that he will be seen for what he is, and what he is depends upon some present knowledge of his past. The same principle holds for societies and nations. They *are* their history, and any detraction from the latter is a detraction from their status. It goes without saying that this history is not simply their spans of existence, but their careers in relation to the "mythic cover." Cultural life depends upon the remembrance of acknowledged values, and for this reason any sign of a prejudice against memory is a signal of danger.

Yet from one point of view it seems foolish to write anything directly about memory. No one appears to know in exact
terms what memory is. Even the most searching of the psychologists today can give us little more than behavioristic description and hypothetical constructs. Still we are faced with
the fact that everyone believes there is such an entity as memory, and there are the reasons given above for insisting that
memory plays a highly important role in cultural ordering. In
another approach to the problem of what is happening to the
synthesis of culture, I shall begin here by listing some things
that indicate a decay of memory.

The slogan today is to forget and live in the future. Wherever
we look in the "progressive" world we find encouragements not
to remember. Increasingly the past is looked upon as a burden.
"Forget it and turn to tomorrow" is the orientation of the times.
People evince in their very manner a pride in letting go of what
has happened and jumping at anything new. The individual conservators of the past exist no more or they are no longer listened
to: the grandmother preserving the history and traditions of the
family by the fireside, the veteran relating the story of his battles
in the shaded courthouse square, even the public orator recalling
the spirit of 1776 on commemorative days. There is no "time" to
listen to them, and time is of the essence. Frederick Wilhelmsen
has summed it up boldly and truly in saying, "history is no longer
a category of the consciousness."[1]

Amnesia as a goal is a social emergent of unique significance. I do not find any other period in which men have felt to
an equal degree that the past either is uninteresting or is a

reproach to them. When we realize the extent to which one's memory is oneself, we are made to wonder whether there is not some element of suicidal impulse in this mood, or at least an impulse of self-hatred. One of the obvious and easy ways to take leave of oneself is to forget, to cease to hold in consciousness what one has been. This is personal annihilation, for no man exists really except through that mysterious storehouse of his remembered acts and his formed personality. His very reality depends upon his carrying the past into the present through the power of memory. If he does not want identity, if he has actually come to hate himself, it is natural for him to try to get rid of memory's baggage. He will travel light. But it will be a deprived land of traveling, cut down to immediate responses to immediate challenges. The element that makes his life a continuum will be missing and in the absence of this he cannot be a human being capable of culture. To be human is to live extensively in two tenses, the past and the future, both of which require for their construction the mind and therefore the memory. We may not be able to say what memory is, but we can say something about its uses. It supplies material for the faculty of reason and it provides the necessary condition of conscience. This is equivalent to saying that it is essential to intelligence and to soul.

Let us state as accurately as we can conceive it the relationship between these attributes and memory.

Beginning with what has actually been observed, we find that no man has revealed high intelligence in any field of activity without a strong and usually an exceptional memory. I refer, of course, to the kind of intelligence we think of as distinctively human and not the quick and simple registration of the presence of an object of which animals are capable. Intelligence on the human level is an ability to perceive things for what they are and to grasp their relationships. Things in these relationships are often not physically compresent. This means that intelligence involves a considerable amount of causal reasoning, which is the linking of phenomena that occur as antecedents and consequents. William James has pointed out that if we are to think of one thing as occurring after another, we must *think* of them both together, and this requires that at least one of the items must be supplied by memory. If we think of striking a match, we must remember that matches are ignited by a process of friction. The mere seeing of a match does not apprise us of this unless we can recall such action or have it explained to us in words before we try the act of striking. Intelligence is this power to associate remembered potencies with things seen simply.

In the world of affairs it has been noted many times that men of extraordinary success have had extraordinary memories. Milton, Napoleon, Mozart, to cite a few examples, had tremendous capacity to retain in memory the subjects of their intellectual passion. And what may be of special significance, men of this kind have a way of remembering details which their inferiors consider too trifling to bother with. Probably that is another proof of the relationships between memory and intelligence, for it is the mark of intelligence to see the ramifications that are possible to the smallest detail. It is certainly true that memory is selective, but the selection proceeds according to lines of penetration into significance. By bringing together the past and the present, an encompassing memory gives one a scope of action. The effective men of the world are not cheerful forgetters but painful rememberers. In general all intellectuality rests upon our power to associate things not present or only suggested by what is present. Thus the intellectual value of anything depends upon our ability to retrieve from memory.

In the more formal definition which psychologists frame, "memory" is "remembering." The intellectual nature of the process becomes clear when we realize that remembering involves learning, recall, retention, and recognition and that discovery of meaning is a help both in learning and recalling. "The wider awake the learner," Robert S. Woodworth has written, "the quicker will be his learning and the slower his forgetting."[2]

Thus the part that consciousness has in our relationship with phenomena is largely a matter of memory. The recollection of uniform lines of cause and effect in the world, the recollection of who we are and of what we are committed to, are equipment for dealing with experience.

It is therefore impossible to imagine a high-grade or effective intelligence without things supplied by the remembering process. We cannot put two and two together without some work of retention and recall. In the absence of "memory traces," however these may be described, no kind of intellectual activity could be carried on by the individual. It seems beyond question then that any attack upon memory, insofar as this metaphor expresses real facts, is an attack upon mind.

For a comparable set of reasons, memory is essential to soul. Soul may be defined, for the purposes of this exposition, as an integrative power binding the individual into an intellectual, emotional, and spiritual unity which is his highest self. I realize that some modern readers will be put off by this term. If they wish to read in its place "psyche" or "personality," these will serve as approximations of what I am dealing with, and the assertions which can be made with regard to them will express the point. If we grant that there is in the human being some such integrative unity, it seems inescapable that memory is essential to it. We have already noted that without memory the individual cannot preserve his conscious identity. Without this he cannot recall his needs of the past, remote and near, which make it obligatory for him to do certain things today. Without memory he would be unable to improve his ethical being because he would have no recollection of those thoughts and acts which left him less than satisfied with himself. He could have no conscience because conscience means conscious self-judgment.[3] If there is one thing that is inseparable from soul, it is an awareness that "this is I doing this." At the heart of soul, to speak figuratively, is responsibility, and responsibility involves widened associations. Moral nature cannot be ordered except with reference to one's identity, which has its formation through history, and this fact is recognized in very practical ways. When an offender is put on probation, he is expected to show, in the probationary period, that he has learned from his misdeeds and that he is consciously framing his life so as not to "forget them" but to be guided away from them. When a convicted man is released from prison, society watches for some time to see whether he will behave himself, and thus prove that he has learned from his errors. In areas that do not involve wrongdoing it takes time to "establish a character." There is point in the saying that youth has no character because it has not had time for the kind of self-direction by which character is formed.

To approach the matter from another side, a fastidious memory is among the first things that we observe in people who impress us as having a soul. They are conscious of their past selves in ways that leave them defined. We feel that there is nothing loose or detached about them; everything they do is notified to the whole being because that being is integrated. That is why we feel in these cases that we are dealing with a person. Memory seems a necessary condition for those lives which have a kind of consistent eloquence in that they are expressive of a point of view and a moral passion. A religious or moral man's first reminder to himself on any critical occasion is to remember who he is. Plato makes the point that even those who have a natural talent for philosophy cannot progress in it unless they have a good memory.

Attitudes like that of the present day toward memory are always referable to general overriding ideas. In this instance we can trace a parallel between the altered view of the world which accompanied seventeenth-century scientific achievement and the altered evaluation of the recollecting process. The effect was to change the concept of memory from that of an active faculty of a special being to that of a passive capacity of a being more and more identified with the physical world. The first great step in this change was the mechanist psychology which began with the philosophy of Thomas Hobbes. This philosopher attempted to dispose of the whole complex subject by declaring that memory is "decayed sense." At once this reduces memory to the status of sensation and makes it subject to a physiological wearing out. Hobbes was followed by John Locke, who saw something more than this in memory, but who nevertheless supported the physicalist conception of it. He admitted that "memory, in an intellectual creature, is necessary in next degree to perception," and that memory is often active, since the mind may turn "the eye of the soul upon some memory image." Nevertheless, his general conception of the mind generated a profoundly misleading idea which lasted until the intensive study given to psychology in our own day proved it fallacious. This was expressed in his famous statement that the mind is "white paper, devoid of all characters." The sensations we get through experience write upon this paper and are the source of the content of the mind. The ideas which make the deepest and most lasting impression are the ones accompanied by pleasure and pain. Other ideas "quickly fade and often vanish right out of the understanding, leaving no more footsteps or remaining characters of themselves than shadows do flying over a field of corn." Locke carried the doctrine further by asserting that the constitution of the body affects this process, since in some persons the brain "retains the characters drawn on it like marble, in others like freestone, and in others little better than sand."

We must realize that a false analogy can be extremely misleading and can produce long-lasting error. People are interested and pleased by the points of correspondence they can perceive; not many will go beyond these to see where the correspondence ceases and to find how many are the points of difference which emerge in a complete comparison. Such has been the consequence of Locke's figure of the mind as a *tabula rasa* and of memory as the endurance of things written on it. So ill-founded is this analogy that a contemporary psychologist has felt it necessary to write: "There is no true analogy to memory to be found in the inorganic realm."[4] Although some present-day psychologists are willing to speak of "memory traces," they admit they have no knowledge as to how these affect the structure of the mind. Something is left there by the process of memory, but how and where we cannot say, and the mind is certainly not a headstone with its inscriptions weathering away with the passage of time.

Indeed, it is now established that forgetting is not due merely to the lapse of time. If forgetting were simply a process of mechanical weathering, the experiences of our youth would be uniformly dimmer in recollection than those of last year or of last week. We know, on the contrary, that certain of an individual's memory pictures, though many decades old, are as clear in the mind as some from the recent past. It is a common observation, furthermore, that people in old age tend to recover the memories of their youth, so that they can relate with more detail something that occurred in their distant childhood than something that occurred but yesterday.

Nor is it true that these memories of long persistence are always produced by strong sensations at the moment. Some of the most vivid memories we have are of certain things to which the name "epiphany" applies. These are objects of mind that seem miraculously endowed with clarity—things caught in a moment of illumination so that they stand forth vivid in form and nature. The image of a companion, of children at play, of a street scene, of a seasonal landscape, will now and then register with a peculiar force and distinctness, as if posed for portraiture, even though we have little personal interest in the subject and are not much agitated in the senses. The scene suddenly arranges itself in some kind of authenticity, and we remember it in a way that cannot be explained through mechanical impression or through our need to remember it.

This suggests that memory has a way of life of its own apart from anything that can be accounted for in physiological psychology. To a great extent memory is under the direction of personality, and this probably explains its high degree of selectivity. People remember what they are oriented toward out of a personal and mysterious complex of needs. There is the kind of man who can spend an entire day with another person without being able to recall the type or even the color of the clothing the other person was wearing. There are persons who have gone to work in the same building for years, but who could give one hardly the vaguest description of the façade of that building. They have "looked" at these things, but they have not become conscious of them in the way that is essential to remembering. A story is told of a certain distinguished professor of philosophy who had to appear in court following a minor traffic accident. One of the questions asked him by the opposing attorney was, "What is the make of the car you drive?" To the infinite merriment of the courtroom he was unable to remember.

I cite these examples to show that memory is not simply the product of repeated association, but of inclination and focus. This points toward the conclusion that memory and the life of the mind are one active process, and that this process is constructive. Impressions endure not simply from the original engraving but from their contribution to the outlook which the individual is forming, this fact explaining the retention in mind of "epiphanies." So memory, intelligence, personality, and soul all seem related, although in a way that may defy further analysis. What we feel justified in saying by way of summary is that memory is active, is selective, and is probably creative. It furnishes the things which we need if "need" is defined in a very broad way, so as to include matters affecting the personality and the spirit of man. This is not to say that memory is a reconstructing of the past to suit our convenience, as some historians have argued that we should reconstruct history. It may, however, mean penetrating more deeply into the significance of past events and in this way altering their status and changing the perspective of the individual.

Usually persons learn things when they set themselves to learn, and correspondingly they remember what they prepare themselves to remember, not when they merely throw themselves open to impressions. As for the opposite process of forgetting, Professor Woodworth believes that is due chiefly to two things: atrophy through disuse and interference. If our memories are not somehow ministrative to what we need to do and to the way in which we need to represent ourselves, or to our desire to integrate our view of existence, they may fade out. The very fact that the process of remembering may strengthen memory points again to the active and constructive employment by the mind of these "traces." In the second case memory may be diminished if there is too much scattering of attention through interference or the competition of other things which break up one's concentration. It should not go unnoticed that recollection means "recollection" or the gathering of things together. Sometimes we say that a person has or has not "recollected himself" in reference to the act of bringing his identity to consciousness. It is just this act of pulling together things which have an attractive nucleus of significance that produces units of identity and meaning. If the individual is too distracted to manage this, we often say that he is "beside himself" or that he is not in possession of his faculties. This is the acute stage of disorganization, but the mild state seems to occur whenever people are less able to concentrate their memories than their highest rational welfare requires.

Despite these actualities, we find today a large and growing cult of presentism, cherished both as an individual credo and as a social philosophy. Presentism, generally defined, is the belief that only existence in the present can give significance to a thing. The passage of time not only retires things from temporal existence but also deprives them of value and meaning. In this belief there is a small portion of truth, which is that the enactment of history renders simple conversion of what is past into the present impossible. But when the concept is applied to ideas, significances, and values, it is manifestly untrue, unless one regards these as simply relative to their times, which no intellectual and moral being can persist in doing. The ideas of past epochs are in some cases more limited than ours; in others they are less so; in any case this is a judgment for the imagination to make and not for the simple sense of historic time. Plato and Aristotle were not, of course, without limitations, but they have told us more about man and society than any two since their time who could be named; Shakespeare wrote before the Enlightenment, but his understanding of tragedy surpasses anything that has appeared since.

The identification of truth and contemporaneity rests upon a false assumption; the present actually has nothing to add to the verity of an idea. The more rigorously this thought is examined, the more justifiable it will seem. For when we come to analyze the real nature of time we are forced to see that the present does not really exist, or that, at the utmost concession, it has an infinitesimal existence. The man who pretends to exist in this alone would cut himself off from almost everything. There is a past and there is a future, but the present is being translated into the past so rapidly that no one can actually say what is the present. If we say that everything should be for the present, we must quickly divorce ourselves from each past moment and at the same time not attend to those subjective feelings, born of past experience, which are our picture of the future. There can be no fulfillment through the mere present. In fulfillment we live in memory with its satisfaction over achievement and in pictures of the future. The richness of any moment or period comes through the interweaving of what has been with what may be. If every moment past is to be sloughed off like dead skin and a curtain is to be drawn upon future probabilities, which are also furnished by the mind, the possibilities of living and of enjoyment are reduced to virtually nothing. So without memory and the extrapolation which it makes possible man becomes a kind of waif, without a home to say he is from or to feel he is going to. Look as they will, the advocates of seeking everything in the present are without a theory. The best they can do is to juggle terms so as to make it appear that what a man wants he can have without assuming responsibility for the past.

In a way sermonizing against "presentism" appears pointless because, as should now be plain, no one actually lives in the present alone. Those who imagine that they do so are but the victims of a faulty analysis. It is possible, nonetheless, to underestimate the harm which can be done by a delusion. "Presentism" may be only a cult founded upon error, but the error can have long life and exert much influence. We should inquire next about what disposes people today to embrace the present with such relief.

A specific resentment arises from the fact that conscience and memory play the role of disciplinary officer. As was brought out previously, these remind us of what we are, what our commitments have been, what expectations we have aroused in others, and so on. It is memory that directs one along the path of obligation. License is checked, or at least made self-conscious by this monitory awareness. Therefore if we wish to be free in the unphilosophical sense of freedom, we must get rid of mind.

Memories inhibit us and even spoil our pleasures. They keep in sight the significance of our lives, which influences and inhibits action. Under the impossible idea of unrestricted freedom, the cry is to bury the past and let the senses take care of the present. It is forgotten that "presence of mind" means "presence of memory." As Jung has pointed out, denial of the past is by no means the same thing as consciousness of the present. But making oneself discontinuous with the past sounds bold and enterprising and makes it appear that one is trusting all to momentary experience. The present is empirical, not conceptual, time.

A part of the temptation, then, is the current impulse in favor of general emancipation, which often consists of striking at restraints without considering what they preserve. In the absence of the identifications which are supplied by memory, the individual becomes Walt Whitman's "simple, separate person." Whitman is notorious for wishing to cast away the baggage of the past; the divine moment in which he was sunning himself on the grass or riding happily in a crowded omnibus was sufficient to itself. His romantic expansiveness wished to be free of old lessons and present obligations. Although there is in this an attractive waywardness, it will hardly stand examination as social philosophy.

To arrive at this naturalistic state of society, we would have to discard those things designated by the term "mind." For this self-isolation and self-reduction of the individual involves a pulling away not only from such of the past as is denominated history, but also from that pattern of rules and restraints by which society is presently represented in our memory. We know through our power of recollection that certain attitudes exist; if we run counter to them, we meet forces which oppose us; if we avail ourselves of them, we accomplish more than we could by an isolated effort. Hence in the actual world those who have the widest consciousness of this complex of forces are best equipped for successful endeavor, and those who have little meet with checks and failures.

This "simple, separate person," however he may be celebrated in romantic lyrics, is not prepared for the world of action and liability. Both his simplicity and his separation are flauntings of mindlessness which do not permit human beings to live together on the basis of cultural contacts.

A second factor behind the cult of presentism is that it serves that curious fetish "adjustment." The term itself signifies adaptation to the physical world and reconcilement to the idea that man is only a part of this. "Mind" has always carried connotations of the transcendental, not to say the supernatural; at least it has always been thought that through mind man cognizes the things that are beyond time and nature. As long as the existence of such an entity was granted, man could not be completely identified with matter. The rhetoric of material progress tells us to put faith in material things, and mind cannot be reduced to matter. So memory, as the content of the mind, falls under disparagement. Every reader of current thinking knows that "merely mental" and "merely subjective" are in general use as derogatory phrases. Therefore what has to be supplied by the mind does not have the same substantive standing as what is presented by the senses. The balance has been tilted so far in this direction that a hidden premise becomes established, and those creations which are products of mind are now treated as ephemeral. When they stand in the way of certain physical adjustments, they are likely to be regarded even as evidences of psychopathology. The trend of this thinking is to say that only those persons who are alert in the way that animals are can be considered adapted to living, and we have already seen the respects in which this narrows down the content of living.

I have mentioned the doubts that ought to occur to anyone who attempts to say, much less to do, something about an entity as hard to define as memory. One has the feeling of coping with a subject which may not even exist in the forms in which he has had to conceive it. Still, if the account which has been of-fered is reasonably true, we are faced with a social fact of great significance, which calls for some kind of countermeasure. If the present general attitude toward memory is harmful, if it does encourage the cultivation of mindlessness, the social critic should propose some countermeasure. Perhaps the best we can imagine, in a situation as difficult as this one, is a rhetoric of coun-terattack. If there is an assault upon memory, we can direct our effort against those forces which are attacking or undermining in the hope of changing the prevailing attitude. The aim would be simple enough: to inspire a more critical attitude toward those things which are inimical to the habit of recollection.

The most effective countermeasure would be to define more exactly the province of science. There would follow from this a change of the outlook which turns in a spirit of helplessness toward science as the arbiter of human life. Not only is physical science by its proper definition and its mode of operation irrelevant to the world of value and feeling, but it also by its very process emphasizes discontinuity. Science as a whole is constantly superannuating itself. But the superannuation of scientific fact is quite a different thing from the accumulation of wisdom. Science can largely forget its past and profit thereby; the individual, to repeat this point, must remember his past in order to preserve his identity and give direction to his life. It is misleading to analogize life with scientific progress. Modern man lives in a world in which the fantastic is ever just around the corner owing to the accelerating technological revolution. He is less inclined to base his thinking on expectations that come from reflecting on history and more inclined to rely on the "miracles" that come with new physical discoveries. This leaves him less in command of his destiny than before because he becomes less well read in human nature, which is the ultimate determiner of what will be done with the findings of science. In brief he is growing inclined to look in the wrong direction for the knowledge of why things happen. Science in the area of human affairs speaks with a false rhetoric, and this step toward redefining the place of science limits the subjects about which it can convincingly argue.

At this point a new formulation of the difference between science and history would be helpful. Science is the study of what is presently true because uniformly true, of what is abstractly true because generally true. History on the other hand is the memory of all the past with all its uniquenesses, as they were expressed in the concrete matter which is creation. Science makes use of memory because we have seen the role of memory in intelligence, but scientific judgments are rational whereas historical judgments are intuitive. That is to say, to the extent that history offers lessons, these lessons appear intermixed with a great deal that is concrete and particular, and the latter have an influence upon the inferences that can be drawn. The insight of a Winston Churchill into the consequences of an historical development when compared with those of a person educated only in scientific rationalism is that of a sage compared with that of a simpleton. Science teaches through validity; history teaches through eloquence behind which lies the persuasiveness of unique historical fact. If science provides experiments, history provides instances, and this is why even folk memories are more prophetic of what will happen than the prognostications of those who have brought the scientific method into the study of social phenomena. The world depicted by science is a world we do not possess and do not even understand except through a difficult effort of conceptualization, but the world of history we possess in a specially intimate way.

This is our reason for saying that although science has its place, history contains science, and it is from the whole that we derive our truest ideas of what is humanly possible. It therefore needs impressing upon the age that as science encroaches and memory is allowed to retreat, man's predictive power regarding the real forces in history becomes fluctuating and uncertain.

Some opposing center against the great modern force of journalism needs to be found. There is in the nature of great

organs of publicity, or in the circumstances which they tend
to bring about, something which causes them to cater increasingly to the sensate. The trend can be pointed out in a number
of ways: first headlines become larger, then the language employed becomes jauntier and less responsible, next pictures
begin to take the place of language, and finally substance itself
is changed to appeal to appetites for the lurid, the prurient,
and the sadistic. Thus the history of journalism has been a
rather steady progress toward sensationalism. At best it seems
that about one or two newspapers in a nation are able to resist
the trend; the others may give in unwillingly, but they say that
surrender is the price of survival. Even magazines once supported by a cultural elite have not escaped this fate. Whatever
may be the complex of causes behind this fact of deteriora-
tion, it can hardly be denied that the new type of publicity is
an encouragement to vivid perception and a discouragement
to philosophical association of ideas. The typical modern news-
paper is an example of ephemera in a sense in which even the
old politically inspired journal was not. These considerations
bring one, of course, in sight of the ancient problem of controlling at the source what can be published, a problem on which
no one should pronounce without giving the most careful
consideration to alternative consequences. It must serve the
purpose here to say that modern publicity is a powerful incen-
tive to short memories, which ought to be counteracted in
some way. It is as if the reader of journalism were to say, "Let
the page retain the perception for me, and give me a fresh
perception tomorrow."

Again the need appears to speak up against the uncritical adulation of youth. It is anomalous that a civilization of long history and great complexity should defer to youth rather than to age. The virtues of youth are the virtues of freshness and vitality, but these are not the virtues that fit one to be the custodian of the culture that society has produced. Deferring to youth is another way of weakening continuity. Mark almost any young person, and you notice that he does not *see* very much, in the sense of understanding what is present to his vision. He perceives, but he does not interpret, and this is because he is too lacking in those memory traces which lead to ideas and concepts. The memoryless part of mankind cannot be the teachers of culture; they are, however, ready learners of it if the real teachers show faith in the value of what they have.

On the positive side, we must re-create in some vivid way the value of historical consciousness. People must be brought to realize that the past has not dropped into nothingness. It is absolutely impossible that the past, because of the fact that it has happened, should be nothing. If it existed only in the form of physiological memory traces, these at least would be *something*. But far more likely is it that the past exists like the enacted scenes of a great drama, permanently recorded in some great memory and pointing up the significance of all that occurs in the "present."

To sum up, there is more truth in saying that the past is the only thing that exists than in saying that the past has no existence. Such theory as we learn from experience is the contribution of the past, and while this is not the only guide to conduct, it would be disbelief in life and creation to dismiss it as nothing. That is why memory is needed to keep us whole and consistent in opposition to that contrary force which is dissolution. Merely a new attitude toward the past as this functional picture should persuade people, even under the dispersive impulses of modernism, not to neglect the highly human faculty of conceptual memory.

FOUR

The Cultural Role of Rhetoric

O ne of the most alarming results of the disparagement of memory is the tide of prejudice which is currently running against rhetoric. Everyone is aware that the old-style orator is no more, and even those speeches which suggest traditional oratory arouse skepticism and suspicion. The discourse that is favored today is without feeling and resonance, so that it is no exaggeration to say that eloquence itself has fallen into disfavor. Moments of great crisis do indeed encourage people to listen for a while to a Churchill or a MacArthur, and this is proof of the indispensability of rhetoric when men feel that great things are at stake. But today when the danger is past, they lapse again into their dislike of the rhetorical mode, labeling all discourse which has discernible emotional appeal "propaganda."

Rhetoric is involved along with memory in this trend because rhetoric depends upon history. All questions that are susceptible to rhetorical treatment arise out of history, and it is to history that the rhetorician turns for his means of persuasion. Now simultaneous with the loss of historical consciousness there emerges a conviction that man should dispense with persuasive speech and limit himself to mere communication. Viewed in the long perspective this must be considered a phase of the perennial issue between rhetoric and dialectic. But great danger lies in the fact that the present attitude represents a victory for a false conception of the role of dialectic in cultural life. States and societies cannot be secure unless there is in their public expression a partnership of dialectic and rhetoric. Dialectic is abstract reasoning upon the basis of propositions; rhetoric is the relation of the terms of these to the existential world in which facts are regarded with sympathy and are treated with that kind of historical understanding and appreciation which lie outside the dialectical process.

The current favor which rational and soulless discourse enjoys over rhetoric is a mask for the triumph of dialectic. This triumph is directly owing to the great prestige of modern science. Dialectic must be recognized as a counterpart in expression in language of the activity of science. We can affirm this, despite certain differences between them, because they are both rational and they are both neutral. The first point we need not labor; the second is important for this discussion because it is the quality of neutrality in science which has caused many moderns to suppose that it should be the model for linguistic discourse.

We hear it regularly asserted that the investigations and conclusions of science are not made to serve *ad hoc* causes. It is usually granted that the scientist is indifferent to the potencies which he makes available. His work is finished when he can say, "Here are these potencies." He is a solver of intellectual problems, as is evidenced by his reliance upon number.

Now, in a fashion similar enough to make the resemblance consequential, the dialectician is neutral toward the bearing of his reasoning upon actuality. The dialectician says, "If you assume these propositions, you must face these implications," and so forth. His work is with logical inference, not historical discovery. If we define dialectic in its pure form, we are compelled to say that it is indifferent to truth, or at least that its truth is something contained in its own operation. Professor Mortimer Adler has pointed out that "truth when it is taken to mean an extrinsic relation of thinking to entities beyond the process of thought cannot be achieved by dialectical thinking."[1] What is said here assumes the possibility of a pure dialectician, and it may be doubted, because of the nature of things, that such a person could exist. But the question I am here pursuing is whether one can become too committed to dialectic for his own good and the good of those whom he influences. I expect to show presently through a famous instance how this can happen.

My thesis is that a too exclusive reliance upon dialectic is a mistake of the most serious consequence because *dialectic alone in the social realm is subversive.* The widespread overturning of institutions in recent history and the frustration man now feels over his inability to guide his destiny begin, at the most profound level, with the disastrous notion that dialectic, unaided by rhetoric, is sufficient for human counsels. We have heard it contended by many leaders of opinion that if man will only avoid emotional approaches and will utilize science in coping with his problems, he will be able to conduct his affairs with a success hitherto unknown. That is to say, if he will rely upon a dialectic which is a counterpart to that of science in arriving at his decisions, he will have the advantage of pure knowledge whereas in the past he has tried to get along with a mass of knowledge and feeling. The point of this chapter will be the contrary: to give up the role of rhetoric and to trust all to dialectic is a fast road to social subversion.

For the introduction of this argument I am going back to the trial and condemnation of Socrates. Certain features of this extraordinary incident will help to illuminate the difficult problem of the relation of dialectic to rhetoric and of both of these to practical policy.

The reflective portion of mankind has wondered for centuries how so brilliant and civilized a people as the Greeks could condemn to death this famous philosopher. It would be blasphemous for anyone to suggest that the Athenian assembly did not commit a dreadful injustice. But since the condemnation occurred, there must have been some cause; and I think the cause lies much deeper than the fact that a few men with whom Socrates associated turned out badly and deeper than the resentment of a few Athenians whose vanity he had wounded through his questioning. The people of Athens had a case against Socrates which can be understood and elucidated. Set against their own attitudes and behavior, the case may not look very good to us, and we can still say that they put to death the most virtuous man in the city. Yet they had a certain cause, possibly more felt than reasoned out, but enough to account practically for the final judgment.

Socrates has come down to us as one of the greatest ethical teachers of all times. But by the Athenians who indicted him he was charged with being a subverter and a corrupter. Before we set down these two ascriptions as wholly incompatible, let us remember that Socrates was also the greatest dialectician of his time. We who study him at this remote date are chiefly impressed with the ethical aspect of his teaching, but those who listened to him in Athens may have been more impressed by his method, which was that of dialectic. By turning his great dialectical skill upon persons and institutions, Socrates could well have produced the feeling that he was an enemy of the culture which the Greeks had created. He was, in one sense of course, the highest expression of it, but the kind of skill he brought to a peak of development needs harmonizing with other things. When a dialectic operates independently of the concrete facts of a situation, it can be destructive. These facts are not determinative logically of the course which the dialectical inquiry must take, but they are the ground from which it must operate in actual discourse. A dialectic which becomes irresponsibly independent shatters the matrix which provides the base for its operation. In this fact must have lain the real source of the hostility toward Socrates. Nietzsche has perceived this brilliantly in a passage of *The Birth of Tragedy*: "From this point onward Socrates conceives it his duty to correct existence; and with an air of irreverence and superiority, as the precursor of an altogether different culture, art, and morality, he enters single-handed into a world, to touch whose very hem would give us the greatest happiness."[2]

We must remember that Socrates begins the *Apology* by telling his auditors that they are not going to hear a clever speaker; that is to say, they are not going to hear an orator of the kind they are accustomed to; if Socrates is a good speaker, it is not in the style of his accusers. They have said nothing that is true; he proposes to speak only the truth. Further along, he professes to be "an utter foreigner to the manner of speech here." Obviously this is not the way in which a speaker consolidates himself with an audience; it betokens alienation rather than identification. Socrates has in effect said at the beginning, "Your way is not my way."

Thereafter Socrates gives an account of the origin of his unpopularity. He had gone around to men who were reputed to be wise and had questioned them about matters of which they were supposed to have knowledge. He found it easy to prove that they were not wise but ignorant or that their knowledge was so confined that it could scarcely be termed wisdom. Among those who underwent his examination were public men, or political leaders, and poets. This story is too well known to readers of the *Dialogues* to need rehearsing in detail. Suffice it to say that Socrates gives a candid relation of how his dialectic had irritated important elements in the population. But it is to the role of dialectic in the defense itself that I wish to direct chief attention. For Socrates, when his life was at stake, could not or would not give up the instrumentality by which he had been offending.

Let us look at the literal charge which has come down to us. "Socrates is a transgressor and a busybody, investigating things beneath the earth and in the heavens, and making the worse appear the better reason and teaching these things to others." Added to this was the further charge that he did not recognize the gods which were acknowledged by the state but insisted on introducing an idea of new spiritual beings. No doubt there are several ways in which this latter charge could have been answered. But the way in which Socrates chose to meet it was exactly the way to exacerbate the feelings of those whom he had earlier offended. It is significant that at one point he feels compelled to say to the assembly: "Please bear in mind not to make a disturbance if I conduct my argument in my accustomed manner." Here is the passage which follows that request:

> SOCRATES: You say what is incredible, Melitus, and that, as appears to me, even to yourself. For this man, O Athenians! appears to me to be very insolent and intemperate, and to have preferred this indictment through downright insolence, intemperance, and wantonness. For he seems, as it were, to have composed an enigma for the purpose of making an experiment. Whether will Socrates the wise know that I am jesting, and contradict myself, or shall I deceive him and all who hear me. For, in my opinion, he clearly contradicts himself in the indictment, as if he should say, Socrates is guilty of wrong in not believing that

there are gods, and in believing that there are gods.
And this, surely, is the act of one who is trifling.

Consider with me now, Athenians, in what respect he appears to me to say so. And do you, Melitus,
answer me, and do ye, as I besought you at the outset,
remember not to make an uproar if I speak after my
usual manner.

Is there any man, Melitus, who believes that there
are human affairs, but does not believe that there are
men? Let him answer, judges, and not make so much
noise. Is there anyone who does not believe that there
are horses, but that there are things pertaining to
horses? Or who does not believe that there are pipers,
but that there are things pertaining to pipes? There
is not, O best of men! For since you are not willing
to answer, I say it to you and to all here present. But
answer to this at least: is there anyone who believes
that there are things relating to demons, but does not
believe that there are demons?

MELITUS: There is not.

SOCRATES: How obliging you are in having hardly
answered, though compelled by these judges! You
assert, then, that I do believe and teach things relating to demons, whether they be new or old; therefore, according to your admission, I do believe in
things relating to demons, and this you have sworn
in the bill of indictment. If, then, I believe in things
relating to demons, there is surely an absolute

necessity that I should believe that there are demons. Is it not so? It is. For I suppose you assent, since you do not answer. But with respect to demons, do we not allow that they are gods, or the children of gods? Do you admit this or not?

MELITUS: Certainly.

SOCRATES: Since, then, I allow that there are demons, as you admit, if demons are a kind of gods, this is the point in which I say you speak enigmatically and divert yourself in saying that I do not allow there are gods, and again that I do allow there are, since I allow that there are demons? But if demons are the children of gods, spurious ones, either from nymphs or any others, of whom they are reported to be, what man can think that there are sons of gods, and yet that there are not gods? For it would be just as absurd if anyone would think that there are mules, the offspring of horses and asses, but should not think that there are horses and asses. However, Melitus, it cannot be otherwise than that you have preferred this indictment for the purpose of trying me, or because you were at loss what real crime to allege against me; for that you should persuade any man who has the smallest degree of sense that the same person can think there are things relating to demons and to gods, and yet that there are neither demons, nor gods, nor heroes, is utterly impossible.[3]

This shows in a clear way the weapon that Socrates had wielded against so many of his contemporaries. It is, in fact, a fine example of the dialectical method: first the establishment of a class; then the drawing out of implications; and finally the exposure of the contradiction. As far as pure logic goes, it is undeniably convincing; yet after all, this is not the way in which one talks about one's belief in the gods. The very rationality of it suggests some lack of organic feeling. It has about it something of the look of a trap or a trick, and one can imagine hearers not very sympathetic to the accused saying to themselves: "There is Socrates up to his old tricks again. That is the way he got into trouble. He is showing that he will never be any different." We may imagine that the mean and sullen Melitus, his interlocutor at this point—nothing good is intended of him here—was pleased rather than otherwise that Socrates was conducting himself so true to form. It underscored the allegations that were implied in the indictment.

This is not the only kind of argument offered by Socrates in his defense, it is true. In fact this particular argument is followed by a noble one based upon analogy, in which he declared that just as he would not desert the station he was commanded to guard while he was a soldier, so he would not give up his duty of being a gadfly to the men of Athens, which role he felt had been assigned him by the gods. Yet there is in the *Apology*, as a whole, enough of the clever dialectician—of the man who is concerned merely with logical inferences—to bring to the minds of the audience the side of Socrates which had aroused enmity.

The issue comes to a focus on this: Socrates professed to be a teacher of virtue, but his method of teaching it did not commend itself to all people. Now we come to the possibility that they had some justice on their side, apart from the forms which the clash took in this particular trial. We have noted that Socrates had derided poets and politicians; and to these the rhetoricians must be added, for despite the equivocal attitude taken toward rhetoric in the *Phaedrus*, Socrates rarely lost an opportunity for a sally against speechmakers. The result of his procedure was to make the dialectician appear to stand alone as the professor of wisdom and to exclude certain forms of cognition and expression which have a part in holding a culture together. It is not surprising that to the practitioners of these arts, his dialectic looked overgrown, even menacing. In truth it does require an extreme stand to rule out poetry, politics, and rhetoric. The use of a body of poetry in expressing the values of a culture will not be questioned except by one who takes the radical view presented by Plato in Book III of the *Republic*. But Socrates says in an early part of the *Apology* that when he went to the poets, he was ashamed to find that there was hardly a man present "who could not speak better than they about the poems they themselves had composed." But speak how? Poets are often lamentably poor dialecticians if you drag them away from their poetry and force them to use explicit discourse; however, if they are good poets, they show reasoning power enough for their poetry and contribute something to the mind of which dialectic is incapable: feeling and motion.

The art of politics, although it often repels us in its degraded forms, cannot be totally abandoned in favor of pure speculation. Politics is a practical art. As such, it is concerned with man as a spatiotemporal creature; hence some political activity must take the form of compromise and adjustment. There is a certain relativism in it as a process, which fact is entailed by the *conditio humana*. But dialectic itself can stray too far from the human condition, as Pericles no doubt could have told him. We need not question that Socrates was an incomparably better man than most of the politicians who ruled Athens. He makes the point himself, however, that had he entered public life, he would have been proceeded against much earlier. That may well have been true, yet one can hardly conclude from its likelihood that human society can do without political leadership. It may be granted too that the men of Athens needed to learn from his dialectic; still they could not have depended upon it exclusively. The trend of Socrates' remarks, here and elsewhere, is that dialectic is sufficient for all the needs of man.

The fact that Socrates had excited the rhetoricians against him is a point of special significance for our argument. We have noted that he liked to indulge in raillery against speechmakers. Now it is one thing to attack those who make verbal jugglery their stock-in-trade, but it is another to attack rhetoric as an art. This is the matter over which the *Phaedrus* arrives at its point of hesitation: Can rhetoric be saved by being divorced from those methods and techniques which are merely seductive? The answer which is given in the *Phaedrus* can be regarded as ambiguous. At the end of the dialogue the rhetorician seems to wind up, by the force of the argument, a dialectician. But no reader can be unaware that Plato has made extensive use of his great rhetorical skill to buttress his case, to help it over certain places, and to make it more persuasive. His instinct in practice told him that rhetoric must supply something that dialectic lacks. This calls for looking further at the nature of rhetoric.

Rhetoric is designed to move men's feelings in the direction of a goal. As such, it is concerned not with abstract individuals, but with men in being. Moreover, these men in being it has to consider in relation to forces in being. Rhetoric begins with the assumption that man is born into history. If he is to be moved, the arguments addressed to him must have historicity as well as logicality. To explain: when Aristotle opens his discussion of rhetoric in the celebrated treatise of that name, he asserts that it is a counterpart of dialectic. The two are distinguished by the fact that dialectic always tries to discover the real syllogism in the argument whereas rhetoric tries to discover the real means of persuasion. From this emerges a difference of procedure, in which dialectic makes use of inductions and syllogisms, where-as rhetoric makes use of examples and enthymemes. In fact, Aristotle explicitly calls the use of example "rhetorical induction," and he calls the enthymeme the "rhetorical syllogism." This bears out our idea that rhetoric must be concerned with real or historical situations, although dialectic can attain its goal in a self-existing realm of discourse. Now the example is some-thing taken from life, and the force of the example comes from the fact that it *is* or *was*. It is the thing already possessed in experience and so it is the property of everyone through the

sharing of a common past. Through examples, the rhetorician
appeals to matters that everybody has in a sense participated
in. These are the possible already made the actual, and the audience is expected to be moved by their historicity.

The relation of rhetoric to "things-in-being" appears even
more closely in the "rhetorical syllogism." The enthymeme, as
students of logic learn, is a syllogism with one of the propositions missing. The reason the missing proposition is omitted is
that it is presumed to exist already in the mind of the one to
whom the argument is addressed. The rhetorician simply recognizes the wide acceptance of this proposition and assumes it
as part of his argument. Propositions which can be assumed in
this manner are settled beliefs, standing convictions, and attitudes of the people. They are the "topics" to which he goes for
his sources of persuasion.

Through employment of the enthymeme, the rhetorician
enters into a solidarity with the audience by tacitly agreeing
with one of its perceptions of reality. This step of course enables
him to pass on to his conclusion. If the rhetorician should say,
"The magistrate is an elected official and must therefore heed
the will of the people," he would be assuming a major premise,
which is that "all elected officials must heed the will of the people." That unsupplied, yet conceded proposition, gives him a
means by which he can obtain force for his argument. Therefore,
quite as in the case of the example, he is resorting to something
already acknowledged as "actual."

Aristotle continues his discussion of the two methods by
pointing out that some persons cannot be reached by mere

instruction. By the term "instruction" he signifies something of the order of logical demonstration. "Further, in dealing with certain persons, even if we possessed the most accurate scientific knowledge, we should not find it easy to persuade them by such knowledge. For scientific discourse is concerned with instruction, but in the case of such persons instruction is impossible; our proofs and arguments must rest on generally accepted principles, as we said in the *Topics*, when speaking of converse with the multitude."[4]

This also puts dialectic in a separate, though adjunct, realm. The mere demonstration of logical connections is not enough to persuade the commonalty, who instead have to be approached through certain "places" or common perceptions of reality. It is these, as we have now seen, which rhetoric assumes in its enthymemes, taking the ordinary man's understanding of things and working from that to something that needs to be made evident and compulsive. As for dialectic, if the motive for it is bad, it becomes sophistry; if it is good, it becomes a scientific demonstration, which may lie behind the rhetorical argument, but which is not equivalent to it.

In sum, dialectic is epistemological and logical; it is concerned with discriminating into categories and knowing definitions. While this has the indispensable function of promoting understanding in the realm of thought, by its very nature it does not tell man what he must do. It tells him how the terms and propositions which he uses are related. It permits him to use the name of a species as a term without ever attending to whether the species exists and therefore is a force in being. That would be sufficient if the whole destiny of man were to know. But we are reminded that the end of living is activity and not mere cognition. Dialectic, though being rational and intellectual, simply does not heed the imperatives of living, which help give direction to the thought of the man of wisdom. The individual who makes his approach to life through dialectic alone does violence to life through his abstractive process. At the same time he makes himself antisocial because his discriminations are apart from the organic feeling of the community for what goes on. By this analysis the dialectician is only half a wise man and hence something less than a philosopher king, inasmuch as he leaves out the urgent reality of the actual, with which all rulers and judges know they have to deal.

The conclusion of this is that a society cannot live without rhetoric. There are some things in which the group needs to believe which cannot be demonstrated to everyone rationally. Their acceptance is pressed upon us by a kind of moral imperative arising from the group as a whole. To put them to the test of dialectic alone is to destroy the basis of belief in them and to weaken the cohesiveness of society. Such beliefs always come to us couched in rhetorical terms, which tell us what attitudes to take. The crucial defect of dialectic alone is that it ends in what might be called social agnosticism. The dialectician knows, but he knows in a vacuum; or, he knows, but he is without knowledge of how to act. Unless he is sustained by faith at one end or the other—unless he embraced something before he began the dialectical process or unless he embraces it afterward—he remains an unassimilable social agnostic. Society does not know what to

do with him because his very existence is a kind of satire or as-
persion upon its necessity to act. Or, it does know what to do
with him, in a very crude and unpleasant form: it will put him
away. Those who have to cope with passing reality feel that neutrality is a kind of desertion. In addition to understanding, they
expect a rhetoric of action, and we must concede them some
claim to this.

In thus trying to isolate the pure dialectician, we have mo-
mentarily lost sight of Socrates. We recall, of course, that he did
not in all of his acts evince this determination to separate himself from the life of his culture. He served the state loyally as a
soldier, and he refused opportunity to escape after the state had
condemned him. His reasoning, in some of its lines, supports
the kind of identification with history which I am describing
as that of the whole man. There is one telltale fact near the very
end of his career which gives interesting if indirect confirmation that Socrates had his own doubts about the omnicompe-
tence of dialectic. When Phaedo and his friends visited Socrates
in the prison, they found him composing verses. A dream had
told him to "make music and work at it." Previously he had
supposed that philosophy was the highest kind of music, but
now, near the time of his execution, being visited by the dream
again, he obeyed literally by composing a hymn to the god
whose festival had just been celebrated and by turning some
stories of Aesop into verse. Perhaps this was a way of acknowl-
edging that a part of his nature—the poetical, rhetorical
part—had been too neglected as a result of his devotion to dialectic and of making a kind of atonement at the end.

Still, the indictment "too much of a dialectician" has not been quashed. The trial itself can be viewed as a supremely dramatic incident in a far longer and broader struggle between rationalism on the one hand and poetry and rhetoric (and belief) on the other. This conflict reappears in the later battle, between Hellenic philosophy with its strong rational bias and Christianity, which ended after centuries in sweeping victory for the latter. Christianity provided all that Greek dialectic left out. It spoke to the feelings, and what seems of paramount significance, it had its inception in an historical fact. The Christian always had the story of Jesus with which to start his homilies. He could argue from a fact, or at least what was accepted as one, and this at once put him on grounds to persuade. We may recall here Aristotle's observation that in conversing with the multitude you do not aim at fresh scientific instruction; you rest your arguments upon generally accepted principles and beliefs, or broadly speaking, on things received. Practically, the victory of Christianity over Hellenic rationalism bears out the soundness of this insight. The Christians have worked through the poetry of their great allegory and through appeal to many facts as having happened, for example, the lives of the saints. Dialectic has been present, because it is never absent from rational discourse, but rhetoric and poetry were there to make up the winning combination.

Hellenic rationalism waned before man's need for some kind of faith and before a pessimism about human nature which seems to develop as history lengthens. We have emphasized that dialectic leads toward an agnosticism of action. Even

Socrates was constantly saying, "The one thing that I know is that I know nothing." The fiercely positive Hebrew and Christian faiths contain nothing of this. As for the darker side of man's nature, what can set this forth but a powerful rhetoric? Dialectic may prove it in a conditional way, but it is up to the elaboration and iteration of rhetoric to make it real and over-whelming. Dialectic alone leads to an unwarranted confidence, and this evidently is the reason that Nietzsche refers to Socrates as an "optimist." If there is one thing which the great preachers of Christianity have inculcated, it is the proneness of man to fall.[5] Without extensive use of the art of rhetoric, they would have been unable to accomplish this. The triumph and continu-ance of Christianity and Christian culture attest the power of rhetoric in holding men together and maintaining institutions. It is generally admitted that there is a strong element of Platonism in Christianity. But if Plato provided the reasoning, Paul and Augustine supplied the persuasion. What emerged from this could not be withstood even by the power of Rome.

One cannot doubt that the decay of this great support of Western culture is closely connected with the decline of rheto-ric. I spoke earlier of a growing resentment against the orator. This resentment arises from a feeling, perhaps not consciously articulated in many who possess it, that the orator is a teacher and a moral teacher at that. He cannot avoid being this if he uses words which will move men in a direction which he has chosen. But here is where the chief point of theoretical conten-tion arises. There are persons today, some of them holding high positions in education, who believe (in theory, of course) that it is improper for any person to try to persuade another person. A name which has been invented for this act of persuading is "psychological coercion," which is obviously itself a highly loaded rhetorical phrase. From some such notion have come the extraordinary doctrines of modern semantics. According to the followers of this movement, the duty of anyone using language is to express the "facts" and avoid studiously the use of emotional coloring. The very use of facts in this kind of context reveals an astonishing naivete about the nature of language. Yet there can be no doubt that this doctrine carries a great danger in that it represents a new attempt of dialectic to discredit and displace rhetoric. The writings of this group contain such a curious mélange of positivist dogma, modern prejudice, and liberal cliches that one runs a risk even in trying to digest it for purposes of analysis. Nevertheless, there are reasons for believing that it is in essence a new threat to fractionate society by enthroning dialectic as the only legitimate language of discourse.

The advocates of the "semantic" approach try to ascertain definitely the relationship between words and the things they stand for with the object of making signification more "scientific." These semanticists believe generally that traditional speech is filled with terms which stand for nonexistent things, empty ideas, and primitive beliefs which get in the way of man's adaptation to environment. For them the function of speech is communication, and communication should be about things that really are. (One cannot read their literature very long without sensing the strong political motivation that inspires their position. A considerable part of their writing is a more or less open polemic against those features of speech which they regard as reflecting or upholding our traditional form of society. At a level below this, but for the same reason, they are anti-metaphysical.) Unless we can establish that the world we are talking about is the world that exists empirically, then, the semanticists feel, we had better not talk at all. They want a vocabulary that is purified of all terms that originate in the subjectivity of the user, or at least they want to identify all such terms and place them in a quarantine ward.

The attempt must be identified as a fresh eruption of pure dialectic because it is concerned primarily with defining. Just as Socrates tried to define "justice" or "love" by now widening, now narrowing the categories, so they try, in a supposedly scientific way, to make the term fit the thing. The two are not engaged in exactly the same quest, and I shall come to their difference later, but they are both relying exclusively upon accurate verbal identification of something that is by them considered objective. As Socrates searched for the pure idea, so they search for the expression of the pure thing or fact. Moreover, they regard this as having the same power of salvation as the archetypal idea.

The quest of semantics cannot succeed, because the very theory of it is fallacious. The connection between a word and what it stands for cannot be determined in the way that they seem to believe. They operate on the assumption that there is some extralinguistic way of deciding what a word should mean, some point outside language from which one can judge the

appropriateness of any choice of words for expression. The effort to get around language and to apply extralinguistic yard-
sticks is doomed to failure even in the cases of words symbolizing physical objects. A word stands for these things, but does
not stand for them in the shape of the things. Language is a
closed system, into which there is only one mode of entrance,
and that is through meaning. And what a word means is going
to be determined by the whole context of the vocabulary, with
all the intermodification that this involves. A word does not get
in through its fidelity to an object, but through its capacity to
render what that object means to us.

But they do not even discriminate rightly the kinds of
things for which words must stand. They assume that all words
must stand for phenomena or things which are observable and
classifiable by science. Indeed, this is their first principle: if a
thing cannot be proved to exist scientifically—if it cannot be
classified *with* phenomena—we are not supposed to bring it
into expression at all, except in those relaxed moments when
we are telling fairy stories and the like. Obviously they are ignoring the immensely important role of the subjective in life.
There are numberless ideas, images, feelings, and intuitions
which cannot be described and classified in the way of scientific
phenomena but which have great effect upon our decisions. A
rhetoric can take these into account, modify, direct, and use
them because rhetoric deals in depth and tendency. A dialectic
in the form of semantics cannot do this because it is interested
only in defining words on the assumption that definitions are
determined by the physical order. Just as the physical scientist

discovers a law or a regularity in nature, so they endeavor to locate the source of terms in physical reality, and indeed their prime concern is to decide whether a referent really "exists." On first thought this might seem to give them the kind of respect for the actual order that I have claimed for believers in history. But a distinction is necessary: history is not the simple data of the perceptive consciousness; it is the experience of man after this has been assimilated and worked upon by the spirit. The appeal to history is an appeal to events made meaningful, and the meaning of events cannot be conveyed through the simple empirical references that semantic analysis puts forward as an ideal. Hence it is that the semanticist too is a neutralist, who would say, "Here is the world expressed in language that has been freed from tendency and subjective coloration." What is to be done with this world is postponed until another meeting, as it were, or it is assigned to a different kind of activity. His great mistake is the failure to see that language is intended to be sermonic. Because of its nature and of its intimacy with our feelings, it is always preaching. This type of agnostic will not listen to the sermon because he is unwilling to credit the existence of values. Yet even after it has been decided that the referent does exist, there is nothing to do with the word except turn it over to others whose horizons are not bounded by logical positivism.

This brings us to the necessity of concluding that the upholders of mere dialectic, whether they appear in this modern form or in another, are among the most subversive enemies of society and culture. They are attacking an ultimate source of cohesion

in the interest of a doctrine which can issue only in nullity. It is
of no service to man to impugn his feeling about the world qua
feeling. Feeling is the source of that healthful tension between
man and what *is*—both objectively and subjectively. If man could
be brought to believe that all feeling about the world is wrong,
there would be nothing for him but collapse.

Socrates was saved from trivialization of their land by his
initial commitment to the Beautiful and the Good. He is also
saved in our eyes by the marvelous rhetoric of Plato. These were
not enough to save him personally in the great crisis of his life,
but they give high seriousness to the quest which he represents.
The modern exponents of dialectic have nothing like these to
give respectability to their undertaking or persuasiveness to
their cause. But both, in the long view, are the victims of supposing that definition and classification are sufficient as the
ends of speech.

In a summing up we can see that dialectic, when not accompanied by a historical consciousness and responsibility,
works to dissolve those opinions, based partly on feeling, which
hold a society together. It tends, therefore, to be essentially
revolutionary and without commitment to practical realities.
It is even contumacious toward the "given," ignoring it or seeking to banish it in favor of a merely self-consistent exposition
of ideas.

Rhetoric, on the other hand, tries to bring opinion into
closer line with the truth which dialectic pursues. It is therefore
cognizant of the facts of situations and it is at least understanding of popular attitudes.

There is a school of thinking, greatly influenced by the Socratic tradition, which holds that it is intellectually treasonable to take popular opinion into account. The side that one espouses in this issue will be determined by his attitude toward creation. When we look upon the "given" of the world, we find two things: the world itself and the opinions which mankind has about the world. Both of these must be seen as parts of the totality. The world is a primary creation, and the opinions of men are creations of the men who live in it. Next the question becomes: can we regard the world as infinitely correctible and men's opinions of it as of no account? Socrates could do this because he believed in a god or gods. The world is by him from the beginning condemned; it is a prison house, a dark cave; it is the realm of becoming which is destined to pass away. All things tend toward realizing themselves in a godlikeness, at which time the mortal and earthly will have been shuffled off. A complete reliance upon dialectic becomes possible only if one accepts something like this Socratic theodicy. But the important point is that it denies the axiological status of creation.

The modern counterpart thinks he can affirm that creation is infinitely correctible because he believes only in man and speaks only on his behalf. When we examine his position, however, we find that he believes only in the natural order. This he reveals by his insistence upon positivistic proof for everything. But from the positive order he cannot draw the right inferences about man. He can find no place for those creations like affections and opinions which are distinctly human and which are part of the settlement of any culture. For him an opinion, instead of being a stage of historical consciousness which may reflect a perfectly bona fide if narrow experience, is just an impediment in the way of the facts. His dialectic would move toward the facts and seek to destroy that which holds the facts in a cohesive picture. On his principle a cohesive or systematized outlook must involve distortion, and this explains why he automatically refers to rhetoric as "propaganda."

In brief the dialectician of our day has no adequate theory of man. Lacking such a theory, he of course cannot find a place for rhetoric, which is the most humanistic of all the disciplines. Rhetoric speaks to man in his whole being and out of his whole past and with reference to values which only a human being can intuit. The semanticists have in view only a denatured speech to suit a denatured man. Theirs is a major intellectual error, committed by supposing that they were going to help man by bringing language under the surveillance of science.

There is never any question that rhetoric ultimately will survive this scientistic attack. The pity is that the attacks should ever have been made at all since, proceeding from contempt for history and ignorance of the nature of man, they must produce confusion, skepticism, and inaction. In the restored man dialectic and rhetoric will go along hand in hand as the regime of the human faculties intended that they should do. That is why the recovery of value and of community in our time calls for a restatement of the broadly cultural role of rhetoric.

FIVE

Forms and Social Cruelty

And has not form two aspects? Is it not moral
and immoral at once; moral insofar as it is the
result of discipline, immoral—yes, actually
hostile to morality—in that of its very essence
it is indifferent to good and evil, and deliberately concerned to make the moral world stoop
beneath its proud and undivided sceptre?

—Thomas Mann, Death in Venice

Throughout the argument thus far I have described culture as an achievement expressing itself in a form and
gratifying by creations that develop in relation to this.
What follows in this chapter will be a reservation or restriction
upon this theme made necessary by the concept of culture as
an affirmation of value. That cultures should be allowed to develop independently and exclusively not only is right, but is
essential; there is a point, however, at which a culture encounters something comparable to "natural law." This is not a law of
nature any more than the natural law of jurisprudence is; it is

a law that derives sanction from a universal consideration of justice. Accordingly what will be said next points to certain bounds beyond which a culture cannot go without transgressing upon the principles which give it liberty.

The reflections which follow have been prompted by a feeling, shared I believe by a good many people, that some cultures create and impose forms which are not worth the cost. These are among the hardest of all things to protest against, since their injustice is one of the hardest things to disentangle from their other effects. There exists no ready position from which one can tell the fellow members of his culture that they are guilty of perverseness in reverencing certain cultural forms. It is even more difficult to say this to members of another culture. Charges of presumption and parochialism can very easily silence one who has not well prepared his ground for the effort. Cultural relativism, as everyone knows, brands the very thought of judgments as silly and hopeless. But to the person who feels that he cannot accept all of the creations and activities of a culture as equally good and that he cannot accept some of them at all, the problem remains a reality which relativistic objections cannot dissipate.

Thus the cultural critic is met at the beginning with the need of a platform from which criticism will be meaningful. In order to achieve a critical vantage point of any kind, he has to be prepared to argue as solidly as he can that not all cultures and not all phases of a single culture have been equally happy for man. He can, indeed, show that this truth is recognized emotionally and practically even by those who deny it theoretically. But once he has broken down this barrier to inquiry, the undertaking presents other difficulties. It is not just a matter of proving his point by weighing the modern New Yorker in a scale with the Polynesian or the New Guinea tribe with the inhabitants of a Swiss canton. Within a single definable culture itself there may be good and bad features, as previously suggested, so that he has to get at the various sources of man's cultural expression which issue in these. He cannot do anything with his findings, however, unless he has decided what it is that he values. Obviously he needs as a sanction for his undertaking a cultural ideal, a concept of man's happiest expression and fullest enjoyment in cultivated living. He can rely only upon formal inquiry by the mind, for polls and questionnaires on such a subject would be supremely ridiculous. He will determine what kind of creature man is in respect to his faculties and what faculties deserve exercise and expression and to what extent. He cannot inquire simply into what will provide the greatest pleasure for the greatest number; the Roman circus no doubt provided pleasure for large numbers through the spectacle of a few wretches being torn to death by animals. Such enjoyment must be excluded on the ground that it is not right even culturally that men should be made to suffer involuntarily so that others can have a pleasure which is ethically revolting. Our true problem then begins to emerge in terms like these. Culture, if we regard it as a harmonious expression of all the powers, has to be credited with a form which can be distorted. A philosophy of culture which is willing to face the fact of value treats as no less serious than factual descriptions the character of the human responses to this highly human creation.

At this point certain threshold factors should be taken into account. It is comparatively unusual for anyone to view his own cultural order with the detachment which makes ethical judgments possible. A person may sporadically condemn this practice or that institution, but it will be done in a spirit of pique or irritation. Resentments do not make one a philosopher of his culture. The great majority of men tend to accept their social and psychic milieu as they accept the physical earth—seeing it as something they have always walked upon and will continue to walk upon. Hundreds of assumptions and acquiescences, many of which date back to our training as a child, condition the attitude which we take toward the surrounding cultural order. Only a few individuals, and these perhaps only with considerable effort, can put themselves in a position to see things stripped of the affinities that develop in a hundred ways. This fact of acceptance is not, as a general thing, to be deplored. It is right that the burden of proof should be upon the dissenting, not the consenting, opinion. Conformance has its beneficial side, since the individual is sustained by his culture much as he is sustained by his set of habits, and it would in most situations only entail a loss to ask him to re-form what has been built up through a long process of growth and learning. All of us are to a large extent thus adapted, and the result is a "way of life," which holds together related activities and makes possible the economy of expectation and fulfillment. On the whole it is best that most men have a prejudice on behalf of their culture which is not easily overturned. It means settlement in their lives, confidence in their way of doing things, and consciousness of status. These things comprise the tradition of a culture, and although tradition is not the sufficient reason for a culture, it is a necessary condition.

The prejudice in favor of one's culture, however, must itself submit to judgment. There are points at which it has to yield, and these points are determined by the criteriological sciences of logic and ethics. I take the position that these have a universal validity so that their conclusions can be used legitimately to criticize the forms of any culture. The assumption denies, of course, the notion that every culture makes its own rules in these areas. Its habitual ways of thinking, yes, and its mores, yes, but these are individual accentuations within the framework of universal criteria. We say that we respect cultures for their differences, but these differences imply an identity, which must be located in some core of humanity. I have stressed the principle in other parts of this work that cultures are self-regarding or centripetal and that it is necessary for a culture to have this kind of independence and selfhood. But such grant of autonomy does not mean that judgments cannot be made among cultures or the various creations of a single culture. To say that a culture cannot be judged would be to say that it has no relation to the realm of value, which is quite the opposite of the truth. Modern social science, especially in the anthropological branch, has partly stultified itself and cast discredit upon its own undertaking by implying that cultural study should disabuse one of any idea of evaluation. For this there was originally a plausible motive, since the less educated classes everywhere show a spirit of narrow condemnation which assumes that anything different from themselves is wrong and even deserving of attack. It was in the interest of scientific understanding and thereafter of social policy to make it more generally known that cultures have their own *raisons d'être* and their own special excellencies. But the combatting of this popular attitude was carried to the unacceptable point of supposing that the expressions of any culture are self-justifying. That this issues in moral and aesthetic solipsism need no proving. On such principle there would be no ground for objecting to the practice of the ancient Ammonites of sacrificing their children to Moloch, or of cannibalism, or of any other indulgence which we are not ashamed to brand as outrageous. It would leave us believing that there is nothing to choose between the culture of sixth-century Gaul and thirteenth-century France; it would force us to say that the culture of the Old Stone Age has as much to teach us as that of nineteenth-century Europe.

It may be true that the objective kind of approach—the *Wertfrei* type of analysis—is useful in discovering and analyzing some lines of cause and effect which are parts of cultural structures. The suspension of the moral judgment is a posture regularly assumed by science in some phases of its investigation. But this is a matter of phase or stage. It is mistakenly assumed by some scientists and by nearly all who are simply infatuated with the idea of science that study can end as well as begin here. Some, of course, admit the necessity of the critical and evaluative phases but think that these are better left to the more general student whom we call the philosopher. However the case, such study will have to be made, for it is not the nature of man in history to sit with hands folded while different pictures of his potentiality and his destiny are being presented. The impulse to say, "This is bad," "This is good," and "This is best" is finally an irresistible and a rightful one.

I begin therefore by rejecting the principle of pure relativism for cultures while accepting that of autonomy. I have elsewhere defined culture as something that satisfies the psychic needs of man. Now either these are general and definable, which is to say they have a nature, or they are not. If they are not, there is nothing which can hold up a prescription for cultures: all is fantasy, whim, and innovation, and study would never uncover anything but an endless series of unique expressions for which there would be no basis of appraisal. It seems much more in line with truth to say that there is a fundamental unity out of which these expressions grow. If certain things are allowed to happen in the substratum, the balance of expenditure and satisfaction is upset, and the cultural expression may produce more pain than pleasure. At this point some kind of correction through criticism and an appeal to the theory of man becomes necessary.

A member of a culture must exercise the right of detached criticism when he feels that some feature of this man-made world in which he lives is productive of cruelty and suffering out of any proportion to the psychic rewards which it furnishes. Some practices impress us as not right, even when they are obvious outgrowths, at certain levels, of the assumptions and precepts of the culture to which we acknowledge allegiance. In the case of other cultures, they are apt to be more quickly discerned. The task in either case is to see how these perversions originate.

Before beginning, however, it is well to heed some important cautions. Pain and suffering are highly individual matters in the sense that it is often dangerous to infer from our own experience how another person or another group is responding to a certain situation. It has been proved that people differ greatly in their tendency to notice pain; one person will be virtually indifferent to what would leave another disabled with suffering. People as groups seem to differ likewise; what is felt as unbearable by one group goes practically unnoticed by another. Different mentalities and psychic dispositions enter into this to complicate the matter still further. Soldiers in the heat of battle have received mortal wounds and have gone unaware of them until the excitement of conflict was past. Ascetics have performed feats of self-denial which would be unthinkable to modern man. What may be called for want of a better phrase the "mental set" of the person makes his sensitivity selective and can virtually deaden some areas of normal human response. The human spirit is more a protean than we commonly suppose; it can assume shapes and accommodate things which we little suspect in our unimaginative hours.

But all this is reservation. To say that the capacity to feel pain is differently distributed and varies with conditions is not to say that pain never occurs, or that one can make no inference about what will cause pain in the generality of human beings. And likewise with groups we are defining as cultures. Not all of the things in the past that we deplore from our present standpoint were felt by the people of that time to be onerous. One therefore has to be both cautious and imaginative in deciding what creations of culture are costing more than the culture can offer remuneration for. But having made this as an utmost concession to the relativist position, we can still affirm that some things are on balance demonstrably bad. This is true also of the forms of high cultures, which is the real subject of this critique.

A culture opens itself to condemnation when it begins to attribute an immanence to the forms and institutions it has created. The source of the evil we are endeavoring to isolate thus lies in a false immanentization. When its products and expressive forms are no longer judged by their referential relations but take on a kind of inner authority and an inevitability, they begin to encroach upon other sensibilities which have their own legitimate roles to play in the life of the spirit. This comes about most commonly when attitudes which properly accompany aesthetic contemplation displace or swallow up attitudes toward something which has a function in the nonaesthetic world. In consequence the object is given an illicit status from which many harms may flow. This can be clarified by a series of examples.

A striking instance which comes first to mind is the high culture of ancient Byzantium. This form-loving order maintained a complex cultural life in that area between the Mediterranean and the Black Seas for nearly a thousand years. The relics of it which remain allow us to see that its life was heavily institutionalized, its religion largely made up of formalistic ritual, and its art expressive of abstract ideals. It was wealthy, and for some it was pleasant, but it was cruel. The oppression of class by class seems to have been bitter and continuous, and its legal punishments were among the most barbarous and inhumane known to history. I think that René Guerdan, in his *Byzantium: Its Triumphs and Tragedy*, has revealed exactly the reason for this. He writes in regard to its capital punishments: "Such terrible executions sprang from the logic of the system: the greater the divinity of the institutions, one might say, the less human the punishments."[1] This brief description might be paraphrased to cover the entire subject of this chapter. Wherever a culture tends to institutionalize and divinize its creations, it begins to levy an excessive tribute upon the human beings for whom these things exist. It falls into the temptation of thinking that there is some principle of immanence in them which justifies extortion, in many different forms, of the people.

Let us move forward to the high point of the medieval period and the glory of Christendom. This era, mistakenly denominated "the Dark Ages" by some people, is one of peculiar fascination. It created one of the most extraordinary social structures of all times, along with a magnificent architecture and other arts which have won the admiration of posterity. When one looks at the religious side of the picture, however, a great darkness appears. It seems to us of the present period almost incredible that many thousands of persons were put to painful deaths because they would not subscribe to certain articles of belief. The amount of suffering which resulted from religious persecution in the Middle Ages was immense. John Fox's *Book of Martyrs* tells that there were in Spain seventeen tribunals of the Inquisition which over a long period of time sent an average of ten persons each to the stake every year, and this is but a sampling of the great toll taken by an undeniably great institution, the Medieval Church. The typical modern man is inclined to see these occurrences as the result of abysmal ignorance or terrible wickedness. He wonders why the Middle Ages could not look beyond their own confines and realize how atrocious these acts would appear to the future.

These people reared great and elaborate institutions; they fell under the spell of them and lost sight of their real meaning. When, therefore, the institutions seemed threatened (it is not well enough known that a chief contemporary defense of the extermination of heretics was the preservation of order), they were given immanent authority and a tribute of sacrifice was offered to them. What had been created in response to the human spirit and had referential justification began to be autotelic and to make its own demands. The forms broke away from the informing impulse and set up an autarchy.[2] The judgment of the world since has been, and I should think the judgment of the world before would be, that this society had some things badly out of adjustment. Great encroachment occurred to the dislocating and the eventual destruction of what had been a great creation. From our perspective in time we feel that the Middle Ages were guilty of human sacrifice, and we do not see that the sacrifice was necessary even for the rightful aspirations of the time.

Let us pass on to the eighteenth century, which was indubitably another peak of European culture, although a very different one in the values it espoused. In manners, social intercourse, literature, and political creations, this was an era of brilliant accomplishment. But with all its elegance of speech, manners, and political life, this society maintained a penal code which was barbarous. Hanging was the penalty for some things which today would scarcely draw three months in jail. For numerous political offenses extreme cruelties were inflicted. Thus on the one hand we see a high level of intellectual accomplishment and a complex code of deportment and social intercourse; on the other hand we see cruel and vindictive punishments for what appear to us rather minor offenses against society. This society averted its face from these victims. What did it feel that it was serving in exacting so heavy a sacrifice? It had come to believe in the immanence of its own elegant forms and was raising them to the rank of an idol. The revolutionary outbreak at the end of the century was wild and disruptive, but we must believe that it was to some extent provoked by this idolization of forms. It went to extremes and finally became enamored of itself, thereby proving our proposition in another way. It is a duty of the student of culture to consider how such corrections can be made less expensively, as well as how situations that bring them about can be forestalled.

Suppose we turn now to our own day and to the monstrosities of similar origin with which we have to contend. It is not stretching the term "culture" beyond what I would include here to call modern Soviet Russia a culture. Russia appears to us as a nation which has committed many dreadful things in a deliberate and systematic way. Even after reports of these have been discounted because of their possible political inspiration, it still appears that the Soviets have practiced what I am terming human sacrifice on a very considerable scale. There occurred the violent liquidation of the old feudal and aristocratic orders during the Bolshevik revolution and the ensuing civil wars. Some years later there occurred mass extermination of the independent farmers—the kulak class—amounting to hundreds of thousands, if reports are to be believed. Then there have been the blood purges and the liquidations of political dissenters following "trials" which have especially offended the sensibilities of the West. All this has happened against the background of a steady stream of exiles to Siberia and the forced labor camps.

Again we must look for the cause of these things not in motiveless cruelty but in the kind of idolatry which sets a form or a creation above its human sources. There is abundant evidence that the Russians have become wedded to a system and a dream of perfection which causes these sacrifices to look like incidental costs along the way. The advocates of "scientific socialism" seized power in 1917. Drawing their ideas from metaphysical and other kinds of philosophical doctrines, they came to believe that there is a destiny for society and that it was their duty to make that destiny a reality. It had the form of an ideal classless regime, served by the collective use of all the means of production and emancipated from what they considered the many false ideas that religion and social tradition had sanctioned.

It appears that the Russians are so fascinated by this political form they have envisioned that they are willing to pay the price, as other societies have paid a high price for other things. It is an engrossment that appears incredible and unpardonable to us who stand outside it, but as there can be no doubt about its general effect, there must be a cause. If the Russians regard Communism as a form with immanent force, we may expect them, on analogy with other societies, to try to justify the expense. This idea has become their god, and they regard it as treason to begrudge the sacrifice. It is the old idolatry, taking a new language, and made more monstrous by the resources of the new technology. Then too there is the bureaucratic aspect.

It is much to be suspected that the oppressive weight of bureaucracy in our time (and in some other times) should be blamed in part upon the formal status that bureaucracy takes unto itself. Everyone who has tried to reform bureaucratic organizations has testified to the difficulty of touching them, to say nothing of cutting them down. The bureaucracy begins to assume an inner justification. Its size, its vertical height with the various strata of authority, and its many offices and channels add up to a form toward which one is invited, if not impelled, to take an attitude of aesthetic reverence. With so many people working together reinforcing each other's effort, and presenting a common front to the world, there arises the image of a great creation. How can anyone strike at a thing so ostensibly designed to serve the needs of the community! To threaten it seems like threatening the very principle that underlies community and culture. The bureaucracy, having acquired this status as another means of survival, endures, even when there is a crying need for its alteration or abolishment. A new entity has come into being to protect it: its formal structure as a thing in itself. By the time the critic has gotten past this, he may be too confused or too exhausted to continue.

But it is by another and very different creation that I wish to test this principle next. It is so unlike the others that at first it may seem startling, but this is where one has to be on double guard. Those cultural manifestations which are near and dear to us usually seem to have a peculiar lightness and indispensability which make us unwilling to classify or even to associate them with practices of the past that we are accustomed to deplore. Obviously this kind of creation is a test of our ability to be both critical and candid.

The most appalling human sacrifice of Western society today is the toll taken by machine culture. As just suggested, our familiarity with these losses has caused us to accept them and to deaden our response to the horror of them. But suppose we make an attempt to see the facts with fresh eyes. In 1960 in this country alone about 38,000 lives were taken by automobile accidents. But we cannot stop with this figure. There occurred along with these deaths tens of thousands of injuries, some of them permanently disabling. The same thing goes on in all of the modern Western countries. A recent Reuters dispatch from London states that since the turn of the century 235,000 persons have been killed on British roads, and the total figure for traffic casualties of all sorts is computed at 7,500,000. To such figures there must be added the numbers taken by airplane

accidents. I do not have statistics for civilian losses, but a statement given out not long ago by the United States Army Air
Force shows that in peace time the annual number of fatalities
from air accidents is about 550 young men—these being, of
course, among the physically finest of the race.

For a moment let us regard this as an empirical fact to be
considered. It is a toll exceeding that of many wars and plagues,
and it is annual. While indeed measures are constantly being
taken in the hope of cutting it down, there is never any thought
of removing the cause. Not long ago Dr. John C. Bugher,
Director of Medical Education and Public Health for the
Rockefeller Foundation, observed that although automobile
accidents kill nearly 40,000 Americans a year, we apparently
consider this to be within reason "for the comfort and convenience of automobiles." Whether the director said this with a
forced expression I do not know, but one can hardly challenge
its truthfulness. It does not conceal the essential horror of this
bargain for "comfort and convenience."

A society should have very strong reasons for being willing
to sacrifice 40,000 lives a year and take care of several hundred
thousand wounded. It certainly does not regard each human
life as infinitely precious if it is willing to trade about 40,000
annually for something that is certainly not infinite. It would
seem, from Dr. Bugher's account, that comfort and convenience, to which we should add a love of mobility, have made
themselves a new Moloch; and the idol demands of his wor-
shippers not only the annual toll of life but also a restlessness
and superficiality of spirit.

Yet there is another factor in the situation. It must be conceded that some of the creations of modern technology are triumphs of form. Their lines are so eloquent and so much ingenuity has gone into them that they seem "beautiful."[3] They appear endowed with a life and a reason for being of their own. The sleek body of the new-model car, the outline of an air transport against the sky—these can be pleasing to the aesthetic sense. Such beauty and utility as they have can easily encourage the feeling that these killers are indispensable. These are examples of tyrannical forms right in our midst, which we find easy to accept and make sacrifice for, even while we deplore the humanly expensive institutions of other cultures.

The air is filled with suggestion that modern Western culture represents a great humanitarian gain over any culture which has preceded it. Yet it would be very easy for some future people to regard ours as one of the most brutal cultures that ever existed. The statistics would be at hand to prove it as well as the stories and the photographs.

Why is it that we are incapable of seeing ourselves as brutal in this indifference? The reason is exactly the same that we descried in other cultures. Speed and power and the formal beauty of the machine are the regions where we have garnered up our heart, and where a people has garnered up its heart, it is singularly blind to anything wrong. If they are asked whether they are not paying an exorbitant price for the thing that is being sacrificed for, they retort, "How would you like to get along without *that*?" referring to whatever it is that is being challenged. The astonishment produced by the question stems from a love of the forms and the feeling of immanent power, which keeps them in an attitude of worship until some power comes along that can overcome this force. We must now consider the source of this power.

The only way in which a culture can protect itself against these growths of perversion is by attaining to a fundamental philosophy of the human spirit, which means that it has to arrive at a true theory of the nature of man. I assume, without feeling it necessary to argue, that man is supposed to be a harmony, that he is happiest when he is in accord with himself. What does "supposed to be" mean in this case? It does not matter for the issue in question whether we think of him as created for a design to be fulfilled, or as under a necessity to express himself in certain ways that are not adventitious in order to achieve that consciousness of physical and spiritual vitality which is happiness in the unsentimental sense. Nor does this need preclude healthful tension and that changing equilibrium which are necessary to his life in history. Both can exist in the presence of essential harmony. I assume further that man universally considered has cognitive, aesthetic, ethical, and religious faculties or means of apprehension. The first is the inquiring faculty, which gives him knowledge; the second, which is essentially contemplative, enables him to enjoy beauty; the third enables him to determine the order of the goods and to judge between right and wrong; and the fourth, which is essentially intuitive, gives him glimpses of his transcendental nature and his destiny.

Unsettlement and evil begin when one of these activities is allowed to invade the sphere of another and to carry on its operation in that foreign sphere. The kind of invasion we have now been considering at some length is conducted by the aesthetic faculty, which finds its satisfaction primarily in form. When a culture has created its forms and has instituted a code of observance, it must, in the absence of the intellectual vigilance mentioned above, fall into an attitude of aesthetic idolatry. The forms are neat and beautiful, and everyone within the culture likes to see them "work," which involves seeing them respected. It is easy to imagine that because they are beautiful and because they seem constitutive, they have immanent value and authority.

This attitude reaches a stage of oppression and cruelty when it supports a reification of forms. For any culture forms are necessary, but the reification of them is a morbid state of formalization. In this condition the forms become separated from good will. They no longer respond with the right immediacy to the exercise of this will, but obstruct it with their self-constitution. The result is that the individual ceases to ask, what are the forms for me? and asks instead, what can I do to subserve the forms?[4]

Looking at the principle involved here, we see that a formal tradition remains good only as long as it makes the due amount of concession to other powers when they are operating in their proper spheres. A form which imposes itself out of rigidity weakens the structure of which it is a part. In social organization this is one of the most widely attested truths. A class maintains itself through an athletic vigor, which enables it to do new things and meet new situations without being shattered like a brittle object.

It even looks for new blood, as we say, restoring itself and keeping its identity while assimilating fresh substance. Those classes which have allowed themselves to become castes and those traditions which have become over-formalized have not proved able to go on functioning as classes and traditions. They have behaved as though their actualization itself were a final end. They have lost sight of the truth that the vitality of a form lies in its ability to go on forming, and this in response to ordered demands of the spirit. But if the lesson is read most plainly in social history, it can be read also in the aesthetic expressions of any culture. Once the forms here have undergone crystallization, the power to respond to new demands is gone.

It can be said that what the spirit aspires to is not the consecration of achieved forms but something more like Aristotle's form of forms. The formalization of forms ends with their actualization in a spatiotemporal medium. But the form of forms is that impulse which causes the forms to go on forming—to go on providing for the life of the spirit without consecrating any one level of forms. Therefore the attitude of the wise toward the creations of their culture will be one of modesty and detachment: "They were good, and they must be surpassed." Any settling down in a belief that the final form has been captured is blindness to the nature of the ultimate process; since it is the function of the forms to go on animating, one can never say, here is the end of accomplishment. Empirically, of course, there will be stops for resting and breathing, and there will be gratification over what has been done, but these are not to be regarded as final attainments. What we are affirming, in sum, is that a realized form must not presume to become dictatorial and repress the life of the spirit by claiming other lands of deference to itself. Hence any granting of moral status and imperative force to form in its spatiotemporal embodiment is a sign of danger. It is the nature of the spirit ever to transcend its outward creations, this being the strenuous necessity of spirituality.

So it is that when a culture falls to the worshipping of the forms it has created, it grows blind to the source of cultural expression itself and may engender perverse cruelty. The degeneration may take the form of static arts, of barbarous legal codes in defense of conventions, or the inhuman sacrifice exacted by a brilliant technology. At some point, its delight in these things has clouded over the right ethical and other determinations of life.

It is much to the point here that certain religions have shown an acute awareness of this danger. They have expressed in their commandments against various things a rooted feeling that beauty may seduce us to step outside "the way." Of all the religions that of the Jews seems to have been most uneasy on the subject of aesthetic indulgence in general. The edict of this religion against graven images, observed even into the present era by all except a few liberal groups, appears in effect a prohibition against the kind of costly involvement which we have been discussing. The traditional Jewish religion is nothing if not moral; it is in fact suffused with an intense and almost fierce spirit of compliance with "the law." The claims of beauty have never made such headway against the "thou shalt not's" of the

Judaic code. A terrible earnestness about the unrepresentable God has conditioned the living and the thinking of the Jew to the almost total eclipse of other things that other religions have not merely accepted but cultivated. It seems to most of those outside it that Judaism goes too far in this respect unless life is to be thought of as something to be entirely occupied by undivided subservience to a moral ideal. With the Jews the fear of the seduction of beauty has amounted almost to an obsession, driving them to unnecessary lengths toward ugliness. The feeling that beauty is evil *in se* reflects some primitive and dark anxiety rather than a free consciousness of what life has to offer. After all this has been said, however, we are forced to admit that it may not be without some root in sound instinct. Like certain other features of this religion, it is a protection, even if an over-protection, against things many peoples have yielded to.

Early Christianity had a very considerable infusion of this spirit. It is sometimes pointed out as significant that the Christian gospels were not written in literary or classical Greek, but in "koine," the common language of the people. It is believed that this language was more consonant with the spirit of Christianity than the highly developed and beautiful language of Greek literature and philosophy. Indeed, if we look back to primitive Christianity in general, we find a large element of protest against the forms of a brilliant culture. The Greeks could out-argue the Christians and the Romans could subject them to their government, but there was in Christianity an ethical respect for the person which triumphed over these formalizations. Neither the beauty of Greek culture nor the grandeur of the Roman state system was the complete answer to what people wanted in their lives as a whole. So we may regard the asceticism and the turning away from beauteous form of early Christianity as a resistance to the kind of encroachment that is defined here.

A similar case is to be observed in our Puritans, who aimed at a recovery of Judaism and primitive Christianity. Everyone knows that the change of religion which they undertook was openly and avowedly a rejection of forms, rituals, and works of art of the Medieval Christian Church. The Church had brought beauty into the service of religion in such a large way that those who journey to Europe today looking for great monuments of art find a majority of them in the products of Catholic Christianity. Whether the Church carried aesthetic indulgence to the point of obscuring and even perverting the true mission of religion cannot be determined here. But it is historically true that many felt it did, and to their feeling we owe the Reformation and the Puritan strain in Protestant Christianity.

This reform moved in the direction of a severe plainness. The Puritans cultivated an Old Testament earnestness about their spiritual state, with a determination to ward off the beautiful and the gracious as means of ingress for Satan. Their sober dress, the dreadful names they gave their children, and the utter simplicity of their chapels amounted virtually to a cult of ugliness. When they were victorious in the English Civil War of 1642–49, they showed no hesitation about closing down the theaters as places where art and the devil consorted. These facts may be branded the excesses of a revolt, yet down to this day there persists in most Protestant churches a kind of aesthetic aridity which is the consequence of this movement. A wholesome morality is inculcated, but beauty is suspect, and the incorporation of forms of worship is still a matter of much concern and debate among the various sects of Protestants.

Again, we may be witnessing the authority of a sound instinct. It was recognized that forms had taken on immanent power, and the decision was to abolish the forms. But the defect of this and of all such movements is that it is only another swing of the pendulum, moving from one extreme to the other. Such movements are irrational reactions to abuses, and we should not have to depend upon them for a settlement of the vexed question of claims. Is there no other way by which, short of accepting the authority of a particular religion, we can draw that line over which regard for the forms of a culture must not step?

Clearly, if the question can be resolved by the intellect, it will have to be undertaken at the level of ontology, where the order of reality is envisaged. Only by appeal to this arbiter can we arrive at a disposition of the different roles of the aesthetic and the ethical. Even so, the problem is obscure enough to have perplexed so great a philosopher as Plato. His attitude toward beauty and the arts has been criticized as contradictory or ambivalent, a charge from which he cannot be wholly absolved. We know that in the *Republic* he gave an explicit decision in favor of the ethical over the aesthetic, banning the poets from his ideal state in a high-handed way which has excited indignation. His charge against them was in essence the charge we have been leveling against the worship of forms: he felt that the poets by playing upon the passions with their depictions created many perverse attachments. Such attachments, though pleasureable, were not in his eyes worth the social cost. Therefore he simply prohibited them. But in finding a solution to the problem, we do not get much more help from Plato than we get from the dogmatic commands of religions.

It was Plato's limitation that he did not produce, nor did he have available, a science of aesthetics such as has been elaborated in the past two centuries from Kant to Croce. His great pupil Aristotle, however, did take one step toward such a science. In his *Poetics* he recognized that art has a function of its own, that it is to be judged by its effectiveness in providing certain kinds of pleasure and not by how well it subserves the state or the individual in their pursuit of the morally good life. In a way Aristotle visualized a separate realm of beauty or enjoyment, and when he turned his attention to conduct, he made this the subject of an independent work, the *Ethics*. One might say that Plato had no safe domain in which to confine the aesthetic activity, but Aristotle found one, just as he "found" certain sciences.

Aristotle's initiative provides perhaps the key to the solution. Somewhere between total prohibition (or as total as could be effected) of the allurements of form because of the preoccupation and sacrifice they entail and complete abandonment to them out of a feeling of their immanent worth which allows us to ignore their ethical consequences, a ground will have to be discovered. But it is not simply a middle ground;

it will be a place which has to be determined by deduction from prior principles.

Let us note that if we adopt Plato's doctrine that art should represent only that which is good because all else created distempers in society, a large portion of what the world has received as art would have to be banned. It would not be possible on such ground to retain the *Iliad* or *The Canterbury Tales* or any of the tragedies of Shakespeare. And this does not take into account the great store of myths on which humanity has drawn for thousands of years, many of which have "immoral" endings, but which are forms of beauty and of instruction in some matters. They were composed not to further any specific moral purpose, but to deepen our vision of what is, to help us to penetrate to the structure of reality and potentiality.

It seems impossible to deny the claim of art to some land of self-sufficiency when we realize that the artist often labors to exclude from our response to his work nonaesthetic demands because these would interfere with his symbolic constructions. He asks that we grant him certain actually nonexistent or impossible situations so that he can produce the apparitions which are art. Just as he tries to keep his realm free from interfering nonaesthetic judgments, so we in preserving the bounds of a different kind of activity may insist that art not try to be regulative in the practical realm. If art is to be granted its proper autonomy, it must show its good faith by giving up its claim to authority where a different kind of activity is required of men. In return for its independence, it enters into a solemn treaty not to encroach upon the rights of neighboring states.

Returning now to the larger theme, we may affirm that the only way a culture can be restrained from "worshipping monuments of its own magnificence" and thereby becoming repressive and destructive even in the midst of splendor is to recognize and preserve these allocations of the spirit. For if man is a cognitive, aesthetic, ethical, and religious creature, he must maintain some rights of office among these various faculties. We have seen how forms may exert a double fascination. Men begin to fall in love with a formalization, which has the effect of providing a second, and unnatural, vindication. What may be a fit subject for aesthetic contemplation, becomes, with slight if any awareness on the individual's part, coercive in the moral sphere. But the sense of beauty or formal gratification cannot be indulged to an extent which deprives the individual or the group of those psychic fulfillments which come through the ethical and religious consciousness.

By the full reach of this reasoning the modern world through its machine culture has fallen into an idolatry no less grave than that of past ages which we are accustomed to censure. Its images differ, but their influence is the same and their tribute is high. We have given grants of power to things which we delight to create and to contemplate, and they abuse us and interfere with our better interests. But the road away from idolatry remains the same as before: it lies in respect for the struggling dignity of man and for his orientation toward something higher than himself which he has not created.

SIX

A Dialectic on Total War

The preceding chapter has dealt with the liability of forms to become oppressive. But manifestly this is the negative aspect of the subject; forms are the result of discipline, as the epigraph also notes, and their role in structuring and sustaining what is created is too omnipresent to require special comment. The next chapter will discuss a situation of the greatest urgency in which the repudiation of forms (not the forming of new forms) has results which are profoundly unethical and which threaten to destroy the foundations of civilization. Form when it is responsible may embody ethical restraint, which is to be distinguished from ethical dictation in the realm of the aesthetic and from aesthetic aggrandizement in the realm of the ethical.

Of the many things which cause us to feel that spirit indispensable to civilization has been weakened, none should arouse deeper alarm than total war. I make no reference here to the enormous physical destruction which the war of unlimited objectives leaves in its wake, terrible as that is. To think in these terms would be to treat it as a merely physical problem, and our means of coping with merely physical problems are increasing all the time. It is easier than ever before to clear up rubble and erect new structures: Western Germany but a few years after the tremendous damage wreaked upon her by punitive bombing was a phenomenon, a veritable phoenix risen from the ashes. The rebuilding of devastated Japan is almost equally impressive and astonishing. Today what man can destroy in this manner he can re-create with great speed. If all we had to think about was how to build new houses and factories where old ones have been obliterated, the emergence of total war as a symptom of our times would not be so frightening. The clay and the stone quarries are there, and it is always possible to rebuild—and sometimes it is a good thing to have to rebuild—provided that the opportunity and the will exist. But what of the opportunity and the will?

As is true of all important developments, the consciousness was prepared for coming of total war some while before it appeared as an actual fact. The theoretical considerations always precede and, in a figurative way of speaking, grade the land for what is to follow. In this case the theoretical preparation was made easier by a general attack upon the idea of discrimination.

For the past several centuries there has been a growing tendency to collapse hierarchy and in consequence to deny, ignore, or abolish proper distinctions among human beings. These distinctions, or discriminations, have been of many kinds, answering to differences in age, in sex, in education, in occupation, in way of life, in degree of commitment to transcendental goals, etc. In periods of high culture, there is interest in diversity as well as in sameness, and society uses the standards of many qualities to measure and identify, not merely the single standard of quantity to weigh. This fact expresses a belief that there are qualities, faculties, and vocations that distinguish human beings in ways that have to be respected. Institutions of all kinds have taken these into account; actually there are very few things that are "the same for everybody," since the giving of the same to different people results in a mechanical and tyrannical repression of special qualities. Society is an articulated system, and articulation requires differences of station and performance.

It was in keeping with this vision of things that even the institution of war up to recent times had to make appropriate discriminations. There were those who were qualified to fight and those who were not; there were those who were liable to its dangers and losses and those who were exempt; there were things which men engaged in fighting a war might do and things they were forbidden to do.

But the theoretical undermining of all discrimination cut the ground out from under discrimination in this area too. The coalescence of the people of a country into one mass, begun under the influence of certain scientific concepts and furthered under the influence of certain sociological and economic dogmas, destroyed the outlook which had given sanction to these discriminations. Those who had insisted that certain groups, by their nature or by their vocation, had a right to be spared the sufferings of war now had nothing to appeal to. The differences on which the appeals had formerly been based were dismissed as illusory or as "undemocratic." Naturally the closer society is moved toward a monolithic mass, the harder it becomes to plead for any kind of exception. One was considered to be like one, and one like all, and this equalitarianism was followed by many corollaries asserting the right and liability to equal treatment. If men are no different from animals, females no different from males, the young no different from the old, philosophers no different from fools, it is easy to proceed on to say that noncombatants are no different from combatants. They are all now fused into one element, which is treated as a unit for the purposes of war—by the country as well as by the enemy.

To say that this change has been brought about by a failure to make distinctions which had become traditional is to state a truth that needs to be recognized, but it is only a halfway stage of the inquiry. Behind this failure itself there must lie some grievous and more pervasive cause, capable of affecting other attitudes. I am confident that we must locate it in the denial that things have independent natures and in the uniform attempt of science since the seventeenth century to explain everything by something lower than itself. This principle is in effect a teleology in reverse; instead of trying to explain things by what they are ultimately aiming at or endeavoring to become, one explains them by pointing out the more primitive or less complex stratum from which they have emerged and on which they are now considered to depend for their being. We are familiar with the general processes in which the mental is reduced to the psychological, the psychological to the physiological, the physiological to the chemical, and the chemical to the physical. Things no longer have natures or wholenesses in themselves, with upward tendencies; they are but configurations of quantities, subject to change by the laws of physical dynamics. As one writer has said: "This establishes a new unity of the universe, but of a different complexion from the Greek one: the aristocracy of form is replaced by the democracy of matter."[1]

Given this as the cosmic view, the democracy of war-making and the democracy of matter are seen to derive from a common ground. "All explanation has to start from the bottom and in fact never leaves it."[2] War is now not a matter of changing minds, but an engineering problem, and an engineer must deal with the basic physical forces. Distinctions among human beings stand above these in the old scale, but in the new scale they stand beneath because the primary being is assigned to the physical.

There is no reason, therefore, why a war measure which is perfected as to means should defer to things that have an inferior standing. Qualities and conditions that differentiate men traditionally now cease to have force. Indeed, the means build up a kind of self-momentum; the more one does, the more one can do, and the frailer become the essences which used to interpose between the world and man's complete manipulation of it. Then a question like "Why did you bomb an open city?" becomes an irrational question. The ontological order with reference to which one could say, "You should not bomb an open city" has passed away. "Open" is now only a

factor in the engineering equation. Thus the world on which
ethical discriminations were based is dissolved into a complex
of lower-order functions.

Now let us turn to the historical evidences of this truth. The
French Revolution marks the period when the impulse to end discrimination and to "integrate" everything first began to make itself
definitely felt. From the beginning of the age of chivalry until this
date the Western world had generally recognized a code of war.
Adherence to it, of course, was not complete, and some shocking
violations can be pointed out, but opinion was against them, and
the concept of total war was not part of the inculcated ethos. The
American Revolution affords a good example of the mentality that
lasted down to and, in some of its phases, after the French Revolution.
The historian Arthur Ekirch has described how the Americans,
"despite the state of hostilities, were able to carry on their normal
peacetime interests and pursuits." His account follows:

> This was not true only of regions unaffected by the
> war, but also applied to civilians caught up between
> the lines of the embattled armies. In an age when total
> war was still off in the future, noncombatants were
> able to enjoy certain rights and immunities. American
> scientists, for example, continued to correspond with
> their colleagues in England. Thus a Harvard scholar
> in a letter to the secretary of the Royal Society in
> London maintained that "political disputes should not
> prevent communication in matters of mere science,"
> nor did he see how anyone could "be injured by such

an intercourse." Benjamin Franklin and other American patriots retained the good will of old acquaintances in England, and to Franklin Sir Joseph Banks, the distinguished naturalist, affirmed: "I respect you as a Philosopher and solicit the continuance of your friendship." Moreover, American students, despite the war, continued to go abroad to study medicine in Scotland, or painting in London under the aegis of the American expatriate Benjamin West.[3]

The Napoleonic Wars following the French Revolution moved a step away from this by bringing in the "democratic" conscript army, but they preserved the distinction between combatant and non-combatant. Civilians retained their freedom of movement. British and French scientists continued their correspondence. The armies marched along paths prescribed for them, fought for victory rather than for annihilation, and expected society to go on with its function. When the eighteen-year upheaval was over, the central figure in it, though overthrown, was neither hanged nor shot. He was transported to an island where he could live out his years in comfort, if not in happiness. When he escaped and repeated his offense, he was transported to a more remote island. There was never any thought of trying to "prove" something by killing him. A distinction was preserved between an enemy on the field of battle and an enemy captured.

During the Crimean War (1854–56) Russia continued to pay interest on its debt to its enemy Britain. War was one thing; the honoring of financial obligations another.

The American Civil War, coming a decade later, marked a decisive turn in the direction of total war. This can be seen in a striking way because in that war both concepts were present: the old chivalric concept of the war of limited objectives conducted against soldiers only and the new one of unlimited warfare involving campaigns against civilians and the total destruction of the resources of the enemy. The Federal Commander George B. McClellan and the Confederate General Robert E. Lee belonged to the old school. Both conducted the type of war which is designed to overthrow the opposing army and decide the issue on the field of battle. It was not part of their policy to turn the war against civilians and non-military objectives. Clifford Dowdey speaks accurately when he writes of McClellan:

> He fought to suppress the armed forces of dissident fellow countrymen whom it was his duty, and his desire, to return to a common Union. He did not consider it his duty, and it was certainly not his desire, to make war on those civilians among his countrymen who differed from him on the interpretation of the Constitution. He fought without hate, without cruelty, as if it were indeed a rebellion to suppress and not an alien people to conquer and despoil.[4]

It was quite possibly for this reason that Lincoln, and especially the Radical leaders of Congress, became impatient with his "slowness," which was the price of his respect for forms, and removed him from command after the Battle of Antietam.[5] The character of the war thereafter changed drastically, and in the last two years the Federal Generals William T. Sherman and Philip H. Sheridan carried on a systematic warfare of destruction in Virginia, Georgia, and the Carolinas with the object of involving the entire population. The statement of the former that he would "bring every Southern woman to the washtub" and of the latter that he had devastated the Shenandoah Valley so that even a crow flying over it would have to carry his provisions sounded the end of the age of chivalry. For his part in this General Sherman has been termed by an admiring biographer a "fighting prophet," who saw beyond the old concept of war to the new order, in which no one and nothing would be spared. That Sherman and Sheridan were prophets is not mere speculation, for we have evidence that their innovations were given attention by the German General Staff. General Sheridan went to Europe as an observer of the Franco-Prussian War. At a banquet given by the German Chancellor in 1870, he remarked that he favored treating civilians with the "utmost rigor," since he believed that "the people must be left nothing but their eyes to weep with over the war." The auditor of this remark confessed himself struck by its brutality, but added that it might warrant consideration.[6] America thus may have helped to teach Europe the "democratizing" of warfare, just as she has taught it a number of other leveling concepts.

Whether the Germans actually put this ideal into practice in the First World War, as the widely publicized "Belgian atrocities" might attest, I do not know. But the advance toward

totalism in this war certainly appears in the sweeping nature of
the conscription practiced by all belligerents and in the way in
which every phase of life—economic, financial, social, and
cultural—was drawn into the struggle and made ancillary to
the war. To an unprecedented degree the idea was promoted
that the nation should become as one, with no thought but to
kill and destroy. Those of mature age may recall the hysteria
whipped up in this country by President Woodrow Wilson,
which went even to the point of banning the playing of German
music.

The Second World War went immeasurably further and
reduced the word "noncombatant" almost to meaninglessness.
Distinctions of sex and age and vocation vanished away. The
Western genius for technology had invented a weapon of destruction which took no account of terrain or of distance—the
bombing plane, which could fly practically anywhere and drop
its lethal cargo on any target that military science or the spirit
of vengeance might suggest.

These obliteration bombings carried on by both sides in the
Second World War put an end to all discrimination. Neither
status nor location offered any immunity from destruction, and
that often of a horrible kind. Mass killing did in fact rob the
cradle and the grave. Our nation was treated to the spectacle
of young boys fresh out of Kansas and Texas turning non-
military Dresden into a holocaust which is said to have taken
tens of thousands of lives, pulverizing ancient shrines like
Monte Cassino and Nuremberg, and bringing atomic annihilation to Hiroshima and Nagasaki. These are items of the

evidence that the war of unlimited objectives has swallowed up all discrimination, comparison, humanity, and, we would have to add, enlightened self-interest. Such things are so inimical to the foundations on which civilization is built that they cast into doubt the very possibility of recovery. It is more than disturbing to think that the restraints which had been formed through religion and humanitarian liberalism proved too weak to stay the tide anywhere. We are compelled to recall Winston Churchill, a descendant of the Duke of Marlborough and in many ways a fit spokesman for Britain's nobility, saying that no extreme of violence would be considered too great for victory. Then there is the equally dismaying spectacle of Franklin D. Roosevelt, the reputedly great liberal and humanitarian, smiling blandly and waving the cigarette holder while his agents showered unimaginable destruction upon European and Japanese civilians.

The object of this reflection, however, is not to place blame for any particular atrocity, but to ask whether civilization has given itself a mortal hurt in going so far beyond bounds that were previously respected.[7]

It is said that some kinds of animals become infected with a type of madness which leads finally to their extinction as a species. Is this the kind of epitaph that will have to be written for modern man if there is anyone left to write epitaphs?

I foresee the objection that this whole problem is being put into false terms by someone who simply does not understand war. It will be said that once you are committed to war, the one and only thing that matters is victory. Your declaration of war is a declaration that another government (or another people, to infer from the present trend) has no right to exist and that any means whatever may be used to destroy them. The sole object is to win and impose your will; all other considerations are impediments or irrelevancies. In times of war military necessity becomes the absolute sanction.

This principle is so terrifying in theory and is becoming so ruinous in practice that we should feel impelled to a re-examination of the "reason" for warfare. The conjoining of "reason" and "warfare," of course, seems absurd to many people. But the phrase itself is not as senseless as at first it might appear. War used to be described in the language of diplomacy as the ultima ratio, the "final resort": what a nation fell back on when all other means of settlement had failed. It implied that you had a logical reason on your side which in the existing situation had to be given the support of force. Moreover, the history of civilized warfare does in fact reflect this rationale of war. The rationale assumes that there is an arbiter of the destiny of nations. The arbiter has often been referred to as God, but even where the idea of supernatural deity was absent, there was some concept of overarching reason which could be depended upon to decide in favor of one party or the other. When a nation had done its best, when it had exerted its maximum *lawful* strength, it accepted the "arbitrament of the sword," whether that was given for it or against it. If against it, the defeated party had to admit that the other side had "the better reason" and had to accept a settlement that accorded with that reason. This is the only way that warfare can be assimilated into the framework of rational thinking. So conceived, war is used as a means of *reinstituting* reason or of bringing people to their senses. Unless war can be conceived in this way, it must be regarded as a completely irrational eruption, and every settlement created by war in the past ought to be cancelled and worked out again in a different way.

But the very fact that war is described as the ultima ratio implies that war is subordinate to reason, not reason to war. Hence what happens when one party decides that this, like other hierarchies, is old fashioned and that the way to conduct war is to carry it *in extremis*? The party then does what nations have done in recent times: it adopts the nondiscriminatory policy and endeavors to make war as complete and as wholesale as energy and ingenuity can manage. Let us try a brief dialectic upon this concept of war.

1. The conventional ways of breaking the enemy's will to resist, which is the object of war, are not meeting with success. Therefore it is concluded that the scope of the war will have to be increased; new methods will have to be brought in and the objects of attack will have to be widened.

2. The enemy soon perceives this, and seeing that the old methods of warfare are being abandoned, he decides that he must not merely follow, but must go the opponent one better. If the war is to be waged with what the Germans called *Schrecklichkeit*, or "horribleness," he feels compelled to try to stay ahead.

3. The inaugurator of these tactics sees this as a new perversity on the part of the enemy and goes still further; having started the "all-out" policy, he is committed to it and cannot pull back without self-condemnation.

4. The enemy, having been forced, as he thinks, to go two steps in this direction, finds it easier to take a third. So he adds to the *Schrecklichkeit* with renewed determination to resist at all costs.

5. And so further. The increase in barbarity goes on until everything is dissolved in blind violence, and there is no desire left but to survive oneself and enjoy the pleasure of destroying and punishing. What started out under the auspices of "reason" now becomes "appetite," a "universal wolf" which must "make perforce a universal prey, and last eat up himself."

This is the theoretical and, as it may happen, the actual end of the policy of "total war." What has occurred in the course of the transformation? The most obvious fact is that war has lost its *character*. By this I mean that it no longer survives as an "institution," which can be described in rational terms, but becomes pure and ultimate unreason. We cannot fit this kind of war into any of the categories that are used in making statements about civilization. To represent this in a figure, war has become a fire so hot that no container will hold it; it will melt anything, and the walls of no furnace are able to keep it within bounds of any utility.

What looked at first like a useful shortcut becomes fatal because it destroys the balance of forces without which things cannot be shaped to man's ends. Only a flaw in thinking, or indeed a failure of the consciousness, could allow the series of steps toward total war to commence. Reliance upon pure and unqualified force cannot in the nature of things achieve a human goal, since in the human realm pure act is destructive.

What are the premises which have launched modern man on a course which, though plausible, must end in this kind of self-defeat? There seem to be two of these, one theoretical and the other expediential.

The theoretical argument holds that you never go to war unless you are absolutely certain that you are right, and that if you are absolutely certain you are right, there is nothing you should leave undone to carry your point. Restraint would be a sign of lack of conviction and considerateness would be laxity. No excuse can arise for not waging the war by any and all means. If you are absolutely right, the enemy has no ground for objecting to anything you do while he is resisting you.

The answer to this, as previously intimated, is that it contradicts the philosophy of war. If war is to have a rationale, it must be an appeal to arbitrament, and arbitrament is a decision. The nation going to war is betting that it is right and is appealing to those forces which, in a morally conceived universe, give strength to the right. "With belief in the right as God gives us to see the right" is the stock formula of any statesman taking his country into war. The critical factor here is the reference to something outside the war itself. It is not that the war-maker makes his right; it is that right warrants the war and enables his side to carry it to a victorious conclusion. The advocate of total war, on the other hand, does not regard victory as something that is up for decision through approved methods of arbitrament, but as something the warring party has from the beginning, or rather would have except for the inexcusable resistance of a totally depraved opponent. So war ceases to be a settlement in the sense of a contest to be decided by the strength and skill of the two sides and turns into a kind of punitive operation, with each one trying to see how much it can make the other suffer in all its parts for refusing to accept the unilateral judgment. Thus total war implies the view that the opponent is altogether evil, not the tragic view of the opponent as a character good in some respects but gone wrong in others, who needs to be "brought to his senses."

In this way total war really undermines the idea of war, and this fact has led some people to favor it. I shall deal with their dilemma in a later passage.

The expediential argument for total war is usually expressed very simply: "It saves lives." I have seen Sherman's campaign in Georgia and the Carolinas defended on the ground that it brought the war to an end sooner consequently saving lives; the dropping of atomic bombs upon Hiroshima and Nagasaki has been excused in the same way. This argument, however, has a fatal internal contradiction. Under the rationale of war, the main object of a nation going to war cannot be the saving of lives. If the saving of lives were the primary consideration, there need never be any war in the first place. A nation threatened by war could surrender to the enemy at once, preventing the loss of even a single life. The enemy would in all probability allow the people of that nation to go on living, even if it demanded "unconditional surrender" and proposed to make the people of that nation slaves. The truth is that any nation going to war tells itself that there are things dearer than life and that it proposes to defend these even at the expense of lives. The people are reminded of this in numberless ways, and every young man is instilled with the thought that he must be willing, if called upon, to make the supreme sacrifice. In war the saving of lives is a consideration secondary to the aims of the war.

This is not to say that there is no economy of means in war. It does, however, say that in war the economizing of lives is not the first aim, since in embarking upon the war that nation declares that the war aims are the supreme goal for which lives will be spent if necessary. The self-contradiction of total war is that it destroys the very things for which one is supposed to be sacrificing. The "total" belligerent finds at the end that he has the formal triumph, but that he has lost not only the lives necessary to win it but also the objectives for which it was waged. In other words he has lost the thing that the lives were being expended to preserve.

Although this view of war may seem to some quixotic, it is required by reason. A nation stooping to wage a war of the total description abandons those discriminations and restraints which civilization slowly and painfully creates through patient example and exhortation. These creations are fragile under the best conditions. It is difficult to bring them into being, easy to shatter them, and they are not readily put back together again. Means and end are related so intimately that means unavoidably have an influence upon ends. After total war, a belligerent is on an immensely lower plane than that on which it began. Means have been "saved," but ends have been changed or forgotten. Conditions in the United States after the Civil War and in Western Europe after the First World War will provide plenty of evidence for anyone who desires historical confirmation of this fact. As for the Second World War, it has ended in a situation in which we make "perpetual war" in order to have a distant "perpetual peace." The means have taken over complete control of the ends.

We are left with neither evidence nor expectation that total war will serve as a deterrent to the making of war any more than the barbarous punishments once inflicted on criminals prevented others from taking up crime. Men are always disposed to meet absolute threats with absolute defiances. Then the war settles down, just as in other circumstances, to a struggle as to which shall prevail, the only difference being greater sacrifice and suffering.

Viewed in another light, this is part of the present world's general exaltation of means over ends. The changes produced by technology offer strong temptation to a well-known human weakness, which is to feel that if you *can* do a thing, you *should* do it. This has reached a point with us where people actually feel a loyalty toward means which leaves them indifferent to ends. The more secular society grows, the more dominant this attitude is likely to become. In the absence of a teleology, which can never be attained except by transcending empirical history, men are thrown back upon seeing how wonderful they can make means in themselves. The mere effort that teleological speculation requires induces many to limit their gaze to means. Furthermore, the temptation to use a means once devised appeals strongly to the child in all of us. If it works well, it flatters our sense of ingeniousness. This is the outlook of the mechanic, and perhaps not even of the very good mechanic. It can never become a statesman, who is charged with accommodating the "institution" of war to the necessities of his people and in the larger purview to the civilization of which they are a part.

Here it is necessary to say something to those who object to regarding war as an "institution" at all and who maintain that the only admissible thought about war is of its total abolition. This position is assumed by many out of a praiseworthy idealism. But when all matters are taken into consideration, how informed and realistic is it? We notice first of all that these people are themselves "totalists," or we might say, total utopians. The only thing they will consent to is a total extinction of war, and some seem to think that the emergence of total war is a step, even though a horrendous and costly one, in that direction. These people are the type of reformers, however, who think that human nature and history can be laid aside.

War is a phenomenon ancient beyond reckoning which has involved man's being in numberless ways. Granted that it is absurd and even criminal to say that "war is the health of the state," still, it is also absurd and it may be unsuspectedly dangerous to say that war is totally foreign to the nature of man. A popular musical review of some years ago contained the refrain, "You have to be taught to hate." This is so far from being true that we can assert, on the contrary, that hating is one of the most instinctive things man does; it is rather the case that you have to be taught not to hate, or at least to control your hatred. In the same way it is false to claim that war is repugnant to man naturally and that men are always tricked into it by the artifices of society or dragooned into it by outside pressure. War appeals to the human spirit in too many ways and too subtly for us to proceed on any such generalization. As an indication of how innate the feeling for war is with us, we may recall that religions show no compunction about using metaphors of war. Consider the way in which the followers of the pacifist Christian religion sing "Onward Christian Soldiers," "A Mighty Fortress is Our God," and "The Son of God Goes Forth to War."

Moreover, it is palpably untrue to assert of any large group that all of its members hate war. All of them may hate it in their moments of most detached and abstract reflection, but how often will these moments occur? A small fraction may hate it sincerely and undeviatingly. But a far larger fraction will be torn between love and hate, between fascination with it as a game and a challenge and revulsion from its consequences. Any political leader preparing his country for war is able to play on this ambivalence. War is "wrong," but just shift the rhetorical framework a little bit and it becomes right and it holds out tantalizing opportunities. This is true even of reputedly great idealists like Lincoln, Wilson, and Franklin D. Roosevelt.

In addition to these there is the significant group which actually loves war. "The mystic soldier" is the name that Kenneth Burke applies to this type in a passage of deep insight.[8] They are the individuals who actually find a mystic imperative in war. They are thrilled by the panoply of the parade, and they derive some intense if obscure satisfaction from the spectacle of slaughter. You cannot lock them up as criminals, for in peacetime they are often quite sober and law-abiding individuals. But unleashed by the emergence of conflict, they are the dogs of war. Nor does it seem that they are abnormal in the sense of degenerates; they appear only to have an unusual development of a strain which is in most men. Every people, including our own, produces the type. General Sherman was certainly one of them. Thomas J. "Stonewall" Jackson, beneath his Presbyterian piety, was another. General George Patton of the Second World War was a good example. You do not get at the nature of such men through the political pressures of a particular hour, since it is not the proclaimed "war aims" which make them want to fight. It is their mystical response to the idea of war itself.

When William James wrote his well-known essay on "The Moral Equivalent of War" two generations ago, he showed an awareness of some of these perplexities. He recognized the deep-lying appeal of the military virtues to human psychology, of which he was, of course, a profound student. He said rightly that we will never be able to disarm the militarists by offering glowing pictures of security and ease, like those proposed by socialists and pacifists. These pictures have no attraction for one side—even though it is the darker side—of our nature.

They have no power to deter these mystic soldiers, who in the course of events often become the leaders, transforming and energizing the masses. The kind of pacifism that rests upon materialistic socialism ignores important areas of the human psyche. But James was himself in error in supposing that human warfare can be converted into a warfare against nature, that we could conscript armies of workers or fighters against nature, give them the same drill, something of the same hardship, and come out with the same result as in war. I fail to see that this would effect the kind of purgation he expected. In warfare we bear against other human beings what Yeats has called an "intellectual hatred." It is a peculiarly deep, bitter, and implacable kind of hatred, growing from the feeling that other *rational* beings have done us wrong. It is nourished by all the powerful emotions: fear of what other rational beings could do to us, pride, honor, dread of humiliation, and thoughts of sadistic pleasure. Is there really any substitute which could drain off this passion? Or at the most, drain off more than the top of it?

In view of all these circumstances, it is delusive to think that war can be abolished totally by some kind of international fiat. Any such notion disregards the ontological basis of war. We are up against something which cannot be dealt with without a clear acknowledgment of the facts which produce it. History indicates that we may be faced with one of that class of things which are going to occupy a certain amount of the ontological order regardless of how we treat them. If we deny them vertical space, so to speak, they are going to find horizontal space. We may imagine that we are getting rid of them when we change their shape or their extent in one direction, but later we find that we have only made a redistribution. There are certain things which we have to come to terms with simply because an attempt at extermination not only fails of its object but at the same time deranges the general settlement. Try to suppress them totally and they only shift their operations and find new modes of existence, some of them more harmful than the previous ones.

Therefore we must ask in all realism whether war is not one of those phenomena which in the nature of its case cannot be just "stamped out." The very attempt to do so shows an ignorance of the kind of force one is proceeding against, which ignorance may give it new opportunities. In recent decades, as just noted, there has been a tremendous sentiment in favor of the total abolition of war. But the general result does not indicate that it has been at all effective, and this suggests that it has not been informed. It has been widespread and it has been vocal, but as far as actual achievement goes, it has been like stabbing the wind. If we take count of the wars that have occurred since the beginning of the twentieth century, we get no impression that war is a moribund phenomenon. Indeed, it is nearer the fact to say that wars are now more frequent, and the prophecy of Nietzsche that the twentieth century would be the classic century of war is well on the way to fulfillment. Let us imagine some citizen born in Dresden around 1890 and educated for a life of culture and refinement in a stable world, as many there must have been. If he is still alive, which is fairly doubtful in view of all that has happened, how must the world look to him? What he must have gone through between 1914 and 1945 is almost inconceivable. A citizen of fallen Rome *ca.* 500 A.D. could hardly have witnessed more of violence, turmoil, and suffering.

We might remember too that this illustration involves one of the most highly developed civilizations in history. In science, in scholarship, and in music no nation of the world had attained more than Imperial Germany. Furthermore, it was internally perhaps the most law-abiding of all nations. These attainments did not save it from terrible destruction in wars, whether these wars were thrust upon it from the outside or started by it out of feelings of insecurity or ambition. This achievement of a high state of civilization alone did not decrease the incidence of war. Some evil force had not been successfully provided against.

Thus the modern war against war has not succeeded, and the failure should suggest a radical revision of approach. The one hope that is left lies in some overriding restraint, some form of limitation upon the war-making impulse itself in its very operation. History affords at least one arresting example of success in controlling war, not by outlawing it entirely, but by canalizing it. This was the institution of chivalry, which flourished from the early into the late Middle Ages, and from which most of our surviving code of war derives. Although chivalry is today the butt of jokes, it was in fact a magnificent formal development. If to the utilitarian mind it appears quixotic, let us remember that quixotism is sometimes the outward aspect worn by precious ideals.

Chivalry was in reality an assertion of the brotherhood of man which makes the abstract, windy, and demagogic apostrophes of the present day to brotherhood look empty. For what chivalry taught is that even when men fight, they must fight as brothers. It was a guarantee of equal and inalienable rights in situations where the passions of men are most likely to deny rights. This, incidentally, is where so much modern theorizing is weak; its solutions might be valid if man were a passionless creature interested only in satisfying a few simple wants (although even this admission of wants contradicts the idea that he is a passionless creature). But see him in all his complexity and ambivalence in a situation where history and rhetoric are playing upon him, and the theories collapse. The people of the age of chivalry seem to have felt, as some no doubt feel today, that it is somehow laid upon man to fight; it is his nature, or his destiny, or his original sin. Fighting could never be abolished, leaving not a trace behind. But they felt that something could be done about the *how*. The code of chivalry declared that even if you feel that you have to fight your brother man, this does not mean that you place him outside the pale of humanity, nor does it mean that you may step outside yourself. Even in warfare, and whether you get the best or the worst of it, you conduct yourself in such a way that civilization can go on. The real, the absolute prohibition, is against shattering the mold of civilization, which includes both you and your foe. Thus under chivalry there existed a spiritual universal dominion, which enclosed the activity of fighting as the furnace walls enclose the fire. It may be countered that it is against all idea of the spiritual for men to fight under any circumstances. But again, we have to deal not with fictitious simplicities, but with the complex and contradictory nature of man as revealed in his historical record. What this particular spiritual motive did was to refine and elevate the practice of war, compelling it to abide by a kind of morality. It may be that in the long and bitter experience of humanity, this is the best that can be hoped for. It will have to be recognized that the worst thing of all is to give up your status as a self-controlled human being, because once that is given up, you are by no means certain of retrieving it. Such is the thought that seems to have lain behind the formal restrictions of chivalry.

Moreover, there is an analogy from civil life which proves that formalism is not always quixotism. Let us suppose that in some community a dreadful crime has been committed, say rape accompanied by murder, and that the criminal has been caught. The facts are generally known; there can be no doubt about who is guilty, and the crime deserves capital punishment. The entire community is aroused and a large public gathering—which we may interpret "mob" if we like—surrounds the jailhouse. Why should not this public gathering, if it represents a majority of the electorate, take the prisoner out at once and give him his due? Execution is going to be his end anyhow, and this action would be quicker, saving both time and money. It would undoubtedly carry out the will of the people, and it would afford the added advantage of "democratic" participation in judgment and execution of the laws. But instead of that there will be observed the tedious forms of law: indictment, trial, judgment, sentence, a wait before the execution, and finally the man is put to death by some legally delegated person. Why go through all this rigmarole to get rid of an infamous criminal? It is the settled opinion in most of our Western world that if society permits the former kind of action to take place, it does harm to itself. There is no substantial difference about the end to be sought. But one means is regarded as anarchical and destructive, and the other as legal and preservative of the mind and structure of society. The forms are expensive, but they are worth more than they cost.

Then there is a further consideration which stays the hand of "direct action." A civilized nation of the Western tradition never says that a criminal, however terrible his crime and however palpable his guilt, has no rights whatever. The very majesty of the law is dependent upon securing to the accused certain rights. These are at the minimum protection against the kind of mass violence just described and trial according to law.

The kind of totalism which denies all rights has been revived in the present age, with its general discrediting of principles and its supposition that the new means entitle us to discard ancient fundamentals of ethics and of law.

No more disturbing symptom of this new mentality has been seen than the demand for "unconditional surrender" recently introduced into warfare. A conception of Franklin D. Roosevelt, the most secular and superficial of all American presidents, it strikes deep at those restraints which in the past kept warfare within bounds. Whether this idea was born of vindictiveness, of which Roosevelt seems to have had an ample portion, or whether it was merely a product of his debonair thoughtlessness is difficult to say. It was a brilliant idea for those who live by public opinion, for it made the kind of display that gets into the headlines and stays there. Yet not only is it blasphemous, it also strikes at the comity of peoples. The brotherhood of peoples, like the brotherhood of men under chivalry, implies some basic sanctions which must not be shattered by the accident of war. The ignoring of these sanctions out of opportunism is a weakening of the fabric itself. The truth of this was illustrated at our expense, when less than ten years after the war was over, we were courting these same "unconditionally surrendered" nations in the hope of making them allies. At what point after unconditional surrender did they become eligible as allies or even as parties with whom any kind of negotiation could be conducted? Or was all this dependent upon the will of the conqueror, who could say according to his whim, "Now you are without the pale," and "Now you are within"? This is of course pure arbitrariness, which cannot be the foundation for any civilized order.

Some may indeed feel that the case against total war is valid up to the recent past but that it collapses in the face of atomic warfare. The invention of super bombs and of intercontinental guided missiles has advanced warfare so near the absolute stage of indiscrimination that even those observances that carried over into our century have been made completely impossible, and nothing seems in prospect but mass brutality. The kind of "reason" that used to underlie the exertion of armed force now fades out as that force is no longer able to respect any distinctions. War, instead of proving some idea, can now only prove that one side has beaten the other to the unleashing of total extermination.

Hopeful consideration must be given here to the thought that there is in humanity something unpredictable and immeasurable that resists the idea of being subjugated by a weapon, however ingenious and powerful. What the unprecedented weapon has always done is to concretize feeling against it on a vast scale, so that its technical superiority is nullified by a great human protest, which brings into the ranks of the opponents large numbers who would not otherwise be there. History furnishes several examples of nations which thought themselves unstoppable because of a "new" or "secret" weapon, but who found that the weapon only multiplied the forces against them, especially the important psychological one. The spirit of man has thus far always prevailed over mere technological means.

The question today, however, is whether we have passed a critical point, so that the effect of the super weapon can no longer be measured in degrees. It approaches the absolute, and once it has been exercised, there is simply nothing left in which opposition can reside. Humanity does not get a chance to re-form its ranks and express its condemnation.

Whether this is so is probably known only to the foremost scientists, or perhaps it is one of the unhatched potentialities of the laboratory.

But if it is true that atomic weapons are now nearly "absolute," the question is whether the spirit of man is capable of forming an attitude powerful enough to prohibit absolutely their use—which would be a step back toward recovering the chivalric concept of limited violence. Our hope seems to lie in the fact that we do know exhaustively the resources of the human spirit. We do not know that in a period of universal chaos it was able to create the institution of chivalry and through it give law to destructive impulses. We do know that more than once in the past the human outlook has undergone even miraculous-seeming changes, so that the ideals of one era completely confounded the expectations of the preceding one. There have been times when men have turned away from all they most sought in a previous age and have sought that which they had held in contempt. Massive as it is, our present infatuation may be susceptible to such a change. The freedom of the spirit is such that, under the guidance of a dialectic and the impulse of a powerful rhetoric, men might turn irrevocably against what now obsesses them and decide that the salvation of happiness requires taking a different course. It seems fantastic, but perhaps not more fantastic than things which have happened. Only a change of this magnitude seems enough to stop the present onrush toward destruction. Only a great conversion, in the sense of turning around, may save us from unprecedented disaster.

With any other conclusion, we have to admit that man has lost control of his destiny. With any other event, we may have to witness the truth of Poe's line, "The play is the tragedy, 'Man.'"

SEVEN

Gnostics of Education

More than any other nation the United States has chosen to look upon its schools at all levels as means of education rather than mere instruction.[1] The difference is an important one, since education means not merely the imparting of information to the mind but the shaping of the mind and of the personality. Instruction may be limited to the transmission of facts and principles it is desirable to know as a body of knowledge, but education is unavoidably a training for a way of life. Education comprises instruction, of course, but it goes beyond instruction to a point that makes it intimately related with the preservation of a culture. Under normal conditions the points of view that an educator instills are the points of view of the culture, and actually nothing else is possible as a settled thing because an education and a culture working at cross purposes can only produce a conflict which has to be resolved. A conflict of this kind of serious proportions has developed in our country with the ascension to influence of the "progressive" theory of education.

There are by now many hopeful signs that the battle has been essentially decided and that the danger carried by progressivism is drawing to an end. The threat of Russian technological rivalry, symbolized especially by the sputniks, and other more healthful pressures may before long produce far-reaching changes in the dominant American educational philosophy. What I propose to discuss in this chapter may therefore before long be history. But since it is the kind of history from which one may learn a great deal about philosophical dead ends and educational follies, the story needs telling in perspective, and the moral needs to be drawn.

It is not too much to say that in the past fifty years public education in the United States has been in the hands of revolutionaries. To grasp the nature of their attempted revolution, we need only realize that in the past every educational system has reflected to a great extent the social and political constitution of the society which supported it. This was assumed to be a natural and proper thing, since the young were to be trained to take places in the world that existed around them. They were "indoctrinated" with this world because its laws and relations were those by which they were expected to order their lives. In the period just mentioned, however, we have witnessed something never before seen in the form of a systematic attempt to undermine a society's traditions and beliefs through the educational establishment which is usually employed to maintain them. There has been an extraordinary occurrence, a virtual educational *coup d'état* carried out by a specially inclined minority. This minority has been in essence a cabal, with objectives radically different from those of the state which employed them. An amazing feature of the situation has been how little they have cared to conceal these objectives. On more than one occasion they have issued a virtual call to arms to use publicly created facilities for the purpose of actualizing a concept of society not espoused by the people. The result has been an educational system not only intrinsically bad but increasingly at war with the aims of the community which authorizes it, as we are now forced to recognize.

Although the history of how this situation came about is not the principal inquiry here, a little background may make the facts seem less incredible.

Public education was an outgrowth of the reasonable idea that a people cannot remain self-governing and free if they are untaught. It grew slowly during the nineteenth century until the coming of industrialism created demands for certain practical branches of it. In this growth few saw anything alarming, except perhaps a tendency to look upon universal literacy as a panacea. At one point in the development, however, there occurred a sinister change. This came about when state bureaucracies were created to set the terms and supervise the working of the expanding public school system. State legislators felt that they had to turn the actual administration of affairs over to a body of "experts." In course of time these state departments of education became virtually autonomous in their power to define the goals, methods, and materials of public instruction.

The final step came when they were able to require all prospective public school teachers through the high school level to take a set number of courses in a subject called "Education," wherein the philosophical premises and aims of the new educators were taught. This is where the doctrinal revolution referred to above really took place. Here was an educational system within the educational system, committed to a body of methodology whose goals were defined by a philosophical sect.

I have said that the new education, for which the name "progressive" has been pre-empted by its advocates, is in marked conflict with our basic traditions and culture. It is not something based upon American experience or European experience or any perceptive view of the history of man. It is rather something dreamed up by romantic enthusiasts, political fanatics, and unreflective acolytes of positive science. These are all people "looking to the future," and the future, as with all who try to protect themselves with this phrase, is their subjective feeling about the way things ought to go. We are told by them that we are "living in a world of change"; but the "catch" is that they are in charge of the change. They are the prophets of the new future, which is going to look very unlike the past.

There is no difficulty at all in specifying reasons for the above charge. I list below some of the chief assumptions and tenets of progressive education. The conflict between them and the principal teachings of the Judeo-Christian-classical heritage of the West will be immediately apparent.

1. There is no such thing as a body of knowledge which reflects the structure of reality and which everyone therefore needs to learn. Knowledge is viewed as an instrumentality which is true or false according to the way it is applied to concrete situations or the way it serves the needs of the individual. Since these educators have embraced the notion that the essence of the world is change, there is no final knowledge about anything. The truths of yesterday are the falsehoods of today and the truths of today will be the falsehoods of tomorrow.

2. This being so, the object of education is not to teach knowledge, but to "teach students." As they translate this into practice, it means that everything should be adapted to the child as child, to the youth as youth, and to the particular group according to its limitations. There are no ideals or standards of performance which these are bound to measure themselves by or to respect.

3. As a corollary of the above principle, the child should be encouraged to follow his own desires in deciding what he should study, and what aspects of what subjects, and at what times.

4. The teacher must not think of himself as being in authority, because authority is evil. The teacher is there as a "leader," but the duty of the leader is

only to synchronize and cooperate with the work of the group.

5. The student should never be made afraid of anything connected with the school. Marks and competitions are bad because they instill feelings of superiority and inferiority, which are "undemocratic."

6. The mind is not to be exalted over the senses: democracy requires that sensory and "activist" learning be valued on a par with intellectual learning. The mentally slow or retarded are not to be made to feel that they are lacking; it is better to impugn the whole tradition of intellectual education than to injure the feelings of the less bright and the lazy.

7. Consequently there should be less education through symbols like language and figures and more through using the hands on concrete objects. It is more important to make maps than to learn them, said John Dewey, the grand pundit of the revolutionary movement.

8. The general aim is to train the student so that he will adjust himself not simply to the existing society, as is sometimes inferred from their words, but to society conceived as social democracy.

A few other propositions equally startling can be deduced from the writings of the new school of educationists, but these should be enough to indicate what a complete reversal the

progressivist theory represents. However, just in case the meaning of this is too revolutionary to reach the consciousness all at
once, let me rephrase two or three of the central ideas.
Knowledge, which has been the traditional reason for institut-
ing schools, does not exist in any absolute or binding sense. The
mind, which has always been regarded as the distinguishing
possession of the human race, is now viewed as a tyrant which
has been denying the rights of the body as a whole. It is to be "de-
mocratized" or reduced to an equality with the rest. Discipline, that
great shaper of mind and body, is to be discarded because it carries
elements of fear and compulsion. The student is to be prepared
not to save his soul, or to inherit the wisdom and usages of past
civilizations, or even to get ahead in life, but to become a member
of a utopia resting on a false view of both nature and man.

This set of propositions practically inverts our traditional
idea of education, which venerates mind, recognizes the moral
and practical value of discipline, and regards competition as
the indispensable spur to outstanding achievement. Yet these
are the very propositions which have been systematically taught
by educationists for about fifty years and which have strongly
affected education on all but the university levels (and even
there in some areas). In fact they have been more than taught;
they have been enforced as dogmas in the schools and departments of education, and more than one prospective teacher has
been advised that he must accept them or be rejected by the
profession.

Where should one look to find the real sources of so profound a revolt against the long-accepted premises of education?

Since we are dealing here with a change of great depth, it seems best not to spend time on intermediate causes, but to look for some major parallel in history and see whether this will not point to the ultimate cause. Progressive education is a wholesale apostasy, involving abandonment of fundamental and long-held beliefs about man and the world. If we are to account for it, we shall have to seek further than the pressures of industrialism and other modern-day phenomena. The analysis will concern basic attitudes toward existence, so that if we search for the root of the progressivist outlook, we shall perforce be dealing with questions of faith and of interpretation of historical experience.

There is one apostasy of a nature and a magnitude to warrant comparison with this one, and it affords a great deal of illumination, even though it happened at a remote time and even though its content cannot be precisely delineated. It was a subversive force in much the same way as our progressivism in education, and although it was finally put down, it lasted long enough to produce a large amount of confusion and to cause the thoughtful to search out its fundamental errors. This was the Gnosticism of the first and second centuries A.D.

Gnosticism may be described as an attempt to reinterpret annalistic Christianity in terms suited to the "enlightenment" of the contemporary era. It was a highly speculative system, which differed from what has become canonical Christianity in two important features: its attitude toward creation, and its doctrine of the nature of man.

According to the Gnostics, creation was not the work of an omnipotent and benevolent creator, but rather of a Demiurge of limited power, who necessarily left it finite and incomplete. Evil was therefore represented by them as congenital with creation. The important consequence of this doctrine was that it taught a dualism of good and evil, in which spirit, represented by man, was good and in which the world at least partly represented evil. Man was therefore superior to the created universe and—although this cannot be set forth in very exact terms—was somehow charged with its improvement. The opponents of Gnosticism, both Christian and neo-Platonic, attacked the Gnostics for the presumptuousness of this attitude toward creation. For example, Tertullian, in his *Five Books against Marcion*, scorned that famous Gnostic for his position on this matter. He wrote: "You, however, are a disciple above his master, and a servant above his lord; you have a higher level of discernment than his; you destroy what he requires. . . . You are an enemy to the sky, and yet you are glad to catch its freshness in your houses. You disparage the earth, although the elemental parent of your flesh, as if it were your undoubted enemy, and yet you abstract from it all its fatness for your food."[2] In much the same vein Plotinus in the *Enneads* criticizes the "human audacity" of the Gnostics. "Two people inhabit the one stately house; one of them declaims against its plan and against its architect, but none the less maintains his residence in it. The other makes no complaint, asserts the entire competence of the architect and waits cheerfully for the day when he may leave it, having no further need of a house."[3] Thus the Gnostics were consistently seen as setting themselves above creation and holding that the material universe, for which they were not responsible, was the real source of evil.

With regard to man himself, the Gnostics taught a doctrine of perfectionism. Man did not require salvation, for he was already in a state of "Messianic blessedness." Since he was in this state, it was not necessary for him to submit to external authority. Gnosticism therefore tended strongly toward antinomianism. This view of the natural blessedness of man, coupled with the feeling of his lack of responsibility for evil, made the Gnostics antiauthoritarian. When they were asked by the Christian Fathers where they got their doctrines, they said that they got them from themselves. As a matter of fact, they taught that every individual has a "hidden Deep," from which there well up thoughts, notions, and impulses. A modern student of the Gnostic movement has noted that this resembles in a number of ways the "Subliminal Self" of modern psychology.[4] We could go on to remark that all this has a parallel in the attempts of our "progressive" educationists to base everything upon psychology.

The decision of the Fathers to reject Gnostic teachings was crucial for the future of Christianity. For the world of the Gnostics was "a fanciful world, 'moulded to the heart's desire,' in which the religious imagination was not tied down to religious facts."[5] Furthermore, such sociology and science as Gnosticism presumed to incorporate were not elements of strength; these consisted of the fashionable doctrines of the day and would have proved an increasing liability with the passage of time. The Fathers were not seduced by the "modernism" of their age. The decision which they made was not only wise for their time but wise for any time in which this kind of choice has to be made. What they did was repudiate theorizing and adhere to annalistic and historical religion. Thus they retained on their side the powerful support of historicity with its facts and traditions. These were of course the fruit of experience, not of conjecture and speculation. The word of a prophet is a deed, it has been said, and they adhered to the word. Debate might range far, but there were always the records, the experiences, and the traditions to return to.

Today we are in a strikingly comparable situation, as enthusiasts and fanciful thinkers call upon us to abandon what we know through the annals of our education and erect a brave new world out of sanguine speculation. Just as the very authority and power of Christianity depended upon rejecting these overtures, so the authority and viability of education today depend upon our rejecting the often plausible appeals of the progressives to give up what we know historically about man and commit ourselves to their utopia.

In sum, it is the contention here that the progressive educationists of our time, while not Gnostics in the sense of historical descent, are gnostics in their thinking. It is a further contention that their gnosticism exhibits the same kind of delusion, fantasy, unreality, and unacceptable metaphysics which the Church Fathers, speaking out of tradition and true insight, challenged and put an end to. Finally, it is my own conviction that the doctrines of the new educationists are at least as menacing to the survival of our culture as were the Gnostic heresies of the first and second centuries to the great religious and cultural tradition which has streamed down to our time. For the essence of Gnosticism is a kind of irresponsibility—an irresponsibility to the past and to the structure of reality in the present. Its teachings cannot serve as the foundations of a culture because the fact that its advocates are out of line with what is, inevitably reveals itself. Where they are allowed to provide foundations, they imperil the whole structure.

The following are a number of specific ways in which our educationists of the new order parallel the Gnostics of antiquity.

Let us note before taking them up that education at any level will reflect the primary assumptions that we make about reality, and for this reason no education is innocent of an attitude toward the existing world. In the way that it explains the interrelationships of phenomena and our relationships toward them, education will reveal beliefs about creation. Even if it denies that the world is something created by a creator, it thereby invokes a theory and prepares ground for an attitude. Of great significance here is the Gnostic account of creation. For the Gnostics, let us remember, creation was the work of a Demiurge who, for lack of omnipotence, had to leave his production finite and incomplete. This doctrine had the effect of introducing a principle of evil (in the sense of incompleteness or a less than perfect realization) with creation itself and of leaving man in opposition to this. Man was good, but creation contained both good and evil, or a world of light and a world of darkness, and the rectification had to come somehow through man himself. On this last point Gnostic theory is somewhat cloudy and confused, but the ideas of a divinized man and a partly evil creation emerge with enough clearness to be considered focal doctrines.

The new educationists do not deal with anything as "remote and academic" (favorite words of condemnation with them) as theories of creation. But they are under the same necessity which requires our ideas to reflect anterior suppositions, and we can gather from their utterances what these suppositions are. For them the universe is not a work of divine omnipotence. All we know about it, they say in effect, is that it is here and that it leaves unsatisfied many of man's wants. This is the reason for holding it bad or incomplete. The completing of it will be brought about through the natural process of evolution plus the efforts that man makes through his science. It is in this reliance upon science and scientism that modern education shows its tendency to hitch itself to a cultural fashion, as Gnosticism showed its disposition to adjust Christianity to a contemporary sophistical world view. Eliseo Vivas has pointed out that "Dewey and his disciples would substitute an education for 'modern man' which instills in the pupil an idolatry toward scientific method and contempt for the achievements of the past, thus fitting him to yield uncritically to the thorough mechanization of his life."[6]

How widely this attitude has been spread through our channels of education can be seen by the frequency with which men now speak of the "conquest of nature." If nature is something ordained by a creator, one does not speak of "conquering" it. The creation of a benevolent creator is something good, and conquest implies enmity and aggression. If by the same token the world is good and is ordained for man, there are certainly suggestions of Pyrrhic victory in the idea of "triumphing" over nature. The man of the new education, however, feels it his duty to be an invader of nature, breaking her "resistance" as in war.

We have just seen how both Tertullian and Plotinus attacked the attitude of scorning that which has been created while continuing to enjoy its benefits. We find further that St. Irenaeus, in his writings against the Gnostics, insists that some mysteries be left unsolved. This expresses the deep feeling, found also in the book of Genesis and in Aristotle, that there are some things it is better for man not to know than to know. Modern man, however, has reached the critical point at which he feels no qualms about demanding that nature give up all her secrets. There no longer exists any doubt in his mind as to whether he is competent to order and dispose of creation. A kind of moral self-modesty which was once present has been lost by his acceptance of a gnostic theory of creation.

A contemporary incident related in the annals of atomic science serves to illustrate this well. Among the observers of the first atomic bomb at Los Alamos in 1945 was William L. Laurence, science editor of the *New York Times*. This correspondent wrote a full account of the terrifying event and closed it, as one would expect a representative modern to do, on a note of jubilation. He told how the group of observers danced with joy following the great flash and boom. "They clapped their hands as they leaped from the ground—earth-bound man symbolizing the birth of a new force that for the first time gives man means to free himself from the gravitational pull of the earth that holds him down." Later, his report goes on to say, one of those present remarked: "The sun can't hold a candle to it." There are two assumptions worthy of note in this passage by the learned science editor. One is that man is the *victim* of the gravitational force that keeps him from flying off into space, and now at last this victim has the chance to do something about his situation. He is going to end this oppression by nature. The other is that man has now improved upon the sun. The original creator did the best he could when he produced this great luminary, but at last man has surpassed him and has made something exceeding it.

At once we recognize how closely this conforms with the Gnostic view that defect lies not in the nature of man, but in the finiteness of creation, which must be overcome by man. The concept of an original disposition for man's good is now made to appear quite archaic. Man is now in the saddle and can ride anywhere.

The connection between this attitude toward creation or nature and the philosophy underlying the kind of school which the Deweyite educators propose is not difficult to discern. The school is of course to be secular because a religious attitude toward the *donnée* of the world is ruled out. Questions of first and final cause are regarded as not within the scope of education, which means that education is confined to intermediate causes. Intermediate causes are of course the subject matter of science, and hence this attitude has the effect of orienting all education toward science. Furthermore, since industrialism is the offspring of applied science, such education fits one ideally for the industrial order. Still further, industrialism is constantly making war upon nature, disfiguring and violating her, and the products of our educational plants can be relied upon to bring the right attitude toward this work.

Of equally evil consequence is the Gnostic attitude toward man, which is, obviously, related to the foregoing. The Gnostic belief was that man is not sinful, but divine. The real evil in the universe cannot be imputed to him; his impulses are good, and there is no ground for restraining him from anything which he wants to do. The mere supposal of such a ground would mean invoking an arbiter which Gnostic thinking does not recognize. By divinizing man, Gnostic thinking says that what he wants to do, he should do. Restraints upon human nature now become blasphemous; whereas in the older thinking it was action of human nature which was blasphemous when it contravened law and ethics. Thus the whole system of ethics becomes man-centered, and there is no sanction above man to which anything can be appealed. What man wants is considered right, and it is what, with the aid of his science, he is supposedly going to get.

I suggest that this radical view of man's nature would never have gained acceptance among so many in this country had not the way been prepared for it by an influential phase of American literature. The New England Transcendentalists of a century ago are a link between ancient Gnosticism and the new gnostic educators. Ralph Waldo Emerson, the leading exponent of Transcendentalism, taught forthrightly that man is divine and that his instincts are oracular. From the "Divinity School

Address" through "Self Reliance" and to "The Over Soul" he developed the theme that man has a divine self-sufficiency and that he does not need to look beyond himself. He instilled in the many thousands who read him as "the American philosopher" belief not only that man bears no responsibility for evil but even that evil is illusory. This was Emerson's rebellion against the Calvinism of his New England forbears, who had taught and acted out of a contrary belief—that man is responsible for the evil which most certainly exists in the world and that he is consequently involved in a curse for which every individual must suffer. As Calvinism with its stern morality and its rigorous intellectualism began to lose ground, its place was taken largely by the expansive optimism which Emerson devised—an optimism which, with its devotion to romantic illusions, was destined to take the sinew out of New England thought and culture.

I mention the Transcendentalists because they, as the most articulate group of radicals in nineteenth-century America, must bear the blame for undermining the previous realism of American thinking. Their influence has been very pervasive, and the progressivist educators have made use of that influence to put forward their heresies as expressive of the American mind and the American political spirit.[7]

We can now safely say that in progressive educational theory we have a gnostic version of the image of man. It is a picture which leaves out of account his original sin, his tendency to love evil and to wreak it, and his daily sinning through egotism. It leaves out of account the dark recesses of his psyche, which even so "modern" a study as psychology has had to restore. The man of the gnostics is the child of his own good nature, confusing his sentiments with the structure of the world, and inclined, when he meets obstacles that do not yield, to blame other men rather than to recognize the limitations of man.

The modern gnostics further resemble the ancient ones in their attitude toward authority. If the ancient type tended toward anti-nomianism, the modern type works toward a theoretical undermining of responsibility. Because human nature is so good that it is not constrainable, laws and traditions are not to be respected. The Gnostics opposed the authority of the Church and the authority of the state under the impulse of their speculative picture of the universe. Again one might mark a parallel with Transcendentalism, for the individual and social protest of Emerson and Thoreau went theoretically to the point of anarchism. Both institutions and traditions were unceasingly attacked by them in the name of the liberty of the individual to follow his naturally good impulses.

The opposition of the present-day gnostics goes about the same length, although for special reasons they do not direct their attack against the state. Many of them seem to carry concealed a Marxist hope that the state may be utilized to gain their ends, after which it will "wither away," or perhaps it will serve as a final target in the attack upon "authoritarianism." As matters stand now, authoritarianism is the principle they chiefly decry. Because all men are equally good, no one is entitled by superior goodness to stand in authority. There are no higher degrees of virtue which authorize some individuals to lay down rules for others. Everybody "cooperates," and what the generality expresses a desire for is what should be done. They overlook the contradiction in this, which is that we always have majorities and dissenters, with the ensuing problem of effecting a resolution. Their position is, however, that no external moral absolute exists by which degrees of rightness and wrongness may be determined. Where no conception of a moral absolute exists, authority has no real basis.

Such are the views implied in the gnostics' dogmatic optimism about the nature of man. As we saw in the historical survey, the ancient Gnostics denied the need of salvation because they considered man to be already in a state of blessedness. Today this translates itself into the doctrine that human beings do not stand in need of correction, to say nothing of conversion. Obviously, if you regard man as already divine, you do not need a discipline for improving him ethically. It has been the general and indeed immemorial practice of the human race to set up some ideal type—"One Perfect Man"—and to judge the moral and intellectual worth of every human being by him. Sometimes the type was presented through religion, sometimes through mythology, and sometimes through the speculations of thinkers. In Christian lands Christ of course serves as the great exemplar and standard. But what the modern educator does is take empirical man, arrive at a type through averaging, and then posit this as what man "ought" to be. What should be merely descriptive thus becomes prescriptive. If you believe that man is already in a "saved" condition, you of course base your ideal on what he generally has been. Then extremes, even of goodness, become "deviants," and need to be pulled back toward the average. The saint is but an eccentric. Such acceptance of man in his average condition must keep down the standard of development and achievement, and the result is a complacency which refuses to believe that man needs to surpass himself.

It is now possible to trace the effects of this system of radical thought upon the education which the progressivists intend to give our children. Not every phase, of course, of the new gnosticism shows a full and equal effect upon educational theory. But that the main tenets of its philosophy exert a strong influence upon the ideals and programs with which we are now confronted becomes clear enough.

First we may turn to the objects of learning. Traditional education has always been based on the assumption that there is a world of data, a fixed reality, which is worth knowing and even worth reverencing. The content of education therefore reflected the structure of an antecedent reality. This, in fact, was education, and everything required for its communication to learners was ancillary. Clearly this presumes a certain respect for the world as creation, a belief in it and a trust in its providence, rather than a view (as if out of ancient Gnosticism) positing its essential incompleteness or badness. The world is there a priori; the learner has the duty of familiarizing himself with its nature and its sets of relations.

Now all of this has been reversed. The main concern of the modern educationists is not knowledge of an existent reality, but rather the mastery of a methodology. The aim of the

methodology is to enable the learner "to grow through experience." These are key terms requiring some examination. The
purpose of education is alleged to be growth, and growth is
conceived as a natural unfolding of the individual. It is not
growth toward something or away from something, because
there are no ideal standards in mind. Sometimes the word
"richness" is brought in to indicate the direction of "growth,"
but it is necessarily and probably deliberately vague. The concealed premise of the doctrine is that the individual is naturally good and that any kind of development of him will therefore be desirable. There is no regulative body of knowledge to
impose a pattern; the individual needs only to increase the
divinity that is in him by the process of growth. As for experience, it need not be qualified; all experience is good and is
more rewarding than knowledge in the abstract. When Dewey
declares that it is more important to make maps than to learn
them, he exalts activity over thinking. While few will deny
that something is gained through the practical handling of a
problem, if the principle of learning solely by doing were applied exclusively, it would cut the learner off from the great
body of traditional knowledge and wisdom of the race. This
he cannot hope to get by experience alone. A number of progressive educators have shown by the trend of their utterances
that they are quite willing to effect such a severance. This
willingness is further evidenced by their attitude toward the
use of symbols. On this subject Dewey has written in *The
School and Society*: "The relegation of the merely symbolic
and formal to a secondary position is not a mere accident but

is part of the larger social evolution."[8] Here as elsewhere one is forced to recognize that these revolutionaries are prepared to state their proposals if not their basic premises in unabashed terms. Their audaciousness, however, should not be allowed to disarm us. What Dewey is insisting upon is nothing less than a denigration of the intellect. For thousands of years education through concepts and the symbols expressing them has been recognized as the education of the mind to which all other education is subsidiary. Through his ability to symbolize and to make use of signs such as letters and figures, man has created practically all that goes by the name of culture. Ernst Cassirer points out that symbol making and using is the most specifically human activity. That culture and civilization depend on an elaborate network of symbols and that the more the human being "advances" the more complex these symbolic media become should be obvious. Now their use is to be de-emphasized in the name of "the larger social evolution," which is a cant phrase standing for the political aims of the progressivists.

It is a strange thing in this day of "progress" and almost universal literacy to have to plead for the rights of the mind, and especially against educators. But as Vivas has shown, the Deweyite school is actually a group of fanatical partisans who are determined to spread their special theory of human nature in opposition to all that history and the humanities have taught us.

The Gnostic belief that man is divine and already in a state of salvation displays itself very clearly in the new theory of "child-centered" education. The upshot of this is not merely to divinize man, which is bad enough, but to divinize the child. The progressivists worship the child as child and make concessions to him where traditional education makes demands upon him. One is compelled to infer from their statements not that the child is the probationer, but that the world of learning is. This is stated by Dewey writing in *Schools of Tomorrow*:

> Are we to believe, with the strict disciplinarians, that education is the process of making a little savage into a man, that there are many virtues as well as facts that have to be taught to all children so that they may as nearly as possible approach the adult standard? Or are we to believe, with Rousseau, that education is the process of making up the discrepancy between the child at his birth and the man as he will need to be, "that childhood has its own way of seeing, thinking and feeling," and that the method of training these ways to what the man will need is to let the child test them upon the world about him?[9]

To commence the reply, why should we believe with the romanticist Rousseau, rather than with the "strict disciplinarians"? It is the experience of most parents and teachers that the child is not a little angel, but in some degree a little savage, and that he needs to be educated out of this condition. There is nothing divine about his imperfections. As for "the man as he will need to be," how do we prepare anyone to become this except by initiating him, with due allowance for his limitations, into the demands and standards of the adult world? Finally, Dewey seems to be overlooking the fact that the real desire of every youngster is "to be a man" and not a perfect little angel of a child.

In *The School and Society* Dewey cites with approval the view of the educator Friedrich Froebel that "the primary root of all educative activity is in the instinctive, impulsive attitudes of children, and not in the presentation and application of external material, whether through the ideas of others or through the senses. . . ."[10] Again like the Gnostics of old, these two see something sacred in instinctive attitudes and in the content of immature consciousness. These are to be venerated above that objectified body of learning which has been produced by systematic study and handed down by our cultural institutions. In brief, learning is to be foregone in favor of the child's spontaneous desires and unreflective thoughts.

Conspicuously absent from all of this is the discipline of the negative. It is invariably assumed that the child can be depended on to develop serious interests without pressure from outside. If this were true, we would have to concede that the child is in a state of grace. The inescapable fact is, however, that the child exhibits no sustained interests or his interests are in trivial or objectionable things. There is no more widely attested fact than that interest usually develops under pressure, and a major part of education consists of our being made to take an interest in things that ought to interest us or will require our interest as we attain adulthood.[11] Effective education often demands the rigorous suppressing of a present, desultory interest so that we can focus on things that have a real, enduring, and sanctioned interest. Indeed, this is identical with the act of concentration. When we concentrate, we rule out the lesser, the peripheral, the seductive interest so that we can get on with the problem we are obliged to solve. I believe it could be demonstrated that progressive techniques of education have done a good deal to lessen the powers of concentration of the present generation of students who have been exposed to them.

This belief in the natural goodness of the child and the lightness of spontaneous expression leads to the progressivists' assault upon virtually all forms of authority and discipline in the classroom. They proceed on the assumptions that fear is never a good thing and that authority must produce fear. There are two important exceptions to be taken to such assumptions. The first is that although authority does sometimes induce fear, it also provides protection, support, and confirmation. It may hold together the organization on which we depend for the exercise of opportunities. Second, not all fear is bad. There are fears that are normal and salutary. We need to fear constantly a variety of dangers, some of which arise from our own nature: we need to fear sloth, carelessness, indifference, and the temptations of appetite. The possibility of ignominy keeps a healthful fear hanging over us, and it is authority which maintains this fear by enforcing the appropriate penalties if we succumb to indolence or to positive evil doing.

Accordingly the gnostics of education feel that they can bring their dream world nearer to reality by introducing "democracy in the classroom." Under this weird conception the teacher is not to be viewed as one in authority commissioned to instruct, but as a kind of moderator whose function is merely to conduct a meeting. Especially resented is the idea that the teacher has any advantage of knowledge or wisdom which entitles him to stand above his students. This would be a recognition of inequality, and equality must reign, *ruat caelum!* The resultant undermining of the authority and prestige of the teacher in public schools is a long story, and the story is now being told by a number of teachers who have experienced it.[12] It is important to show the theoretical objections to this "democratic" maneuver.

Not only is the teacher supposed to be apologetic about his superior knowledge, he is expected to give up one of the most valuable of pedagogical devices, which is the dramatic confrontation of master and pupil. Our traditional means of education has a most important resource in this situation. That one is admitted to be master and the other learner is a circumstance of good effect because it works to tone up the performance of both—the teacher stays on his toes trying to justify by superior knowledge and skill the office that is vested in him; the learner tries to earn the good opinion of the teacher by matching his performance as nearly as he can. In this way a vital tension is set up, and the powerful force of emulation is brought into play. The teacher is going to give the best that he has, and he is going to ask the ordinary mortal sitting there in row three to rise above his ordinary mortality and to excel. A healthful rivalry thus creates standards of criticism.

How the progressivists expect to compensate for this with a kind of relaxed, "democratic," shoulder-rubbing camaraderie in which the teacher is just "one of the boys" is another mystery of the assault upon criteria; for the teacher requires the magisterial stance in order to get the most from his pupils. The old New Englanders, although they developed a number of democratic forms, knew where democracy was in place and where not. The ministers of their churches they called "teachers," and the teacher in the school was a kind of minister in the classroom. There was no sentimental blurring of the roles of instructor and learner. I suspect the fact that New England had thus established a firm intellectual tradition enabled the gnostic thinkers, when they came into ascendancy there, to exert much more influence than their doctrines otherwise would have secured for them.

In review, we see in this startling revolution the substitution of fantasy for historicity. Not only the traditional educator but also the "man in the street" when he is apprised of these facts knows that the progressive educators are not dealing in truth. The reason is that they have set themselves up as Messianic prophets, whose prophecy is of a special political world; therefore they are not primarily educators. An educator is a man inspired with deference toward the world's knowledge and prepared to communicate some phase of it to oncoming generations. One does not have to strip off many wrappings to see that the progressive educators are, by contrast, political ideologues. They are determined to destroy the organic society which we have inherited by postulating an equalitarian natural man as the grand end of all endeavor. Appreciating this fact enables us to understand their attack upon discipline and authority, their opposition to systems of grading and promotion, and their resistance to formal intellectual learning. Almost any question about their assumptions and their methods, if pushed far enough, will bring the defense that these are vindicated by their contribution to democracy. Their writings are filled with references to democracy as a "way of life." This in turn has led to strange cant about "education for democratic living."

There are several things to be said about this piece of sentimental affectation. For one thing, as we have pointed out elsewhere, democracy is not a way of life but a form of government. Government is not the substance of a people's life, although modern collectivism would persuade us to think so. Government in all free societies is a regulative machinery, whose task it is to provide protection and to preserve enough order for people to do what they can do for themselves as individual members of society. This identification of democracy with life is a rhetorical way of sneaking in the totalitarian concept.

For another, democracy is not the only conceivable form of government, although it has virtually become dogma to say so. It was not so regarded by Aristotle, who made aim rather than form the criterion of true government. The most that can be said is that democracy seems to be the best of the available choices for us today, and it is well for the student to be taught in what ways democracy is practical for us. But training for a form of government is neither the sole nor the primary object of education. Man may, by one classification, be a political animal, but political activity is not his highest expression. He is also a contemplative animal, and a creature with aesthetic and cultural yearnings. His very restlessness is a sign that he is a spiritual being with intimations about his origin and destiny. The matters with which education should deal include all these and not merely his political orientation and allegiance. Liberal education has flourished under and contributed to many forms of government, although there may be grave doubt as to whether it is compatible with the current concept of mass democracy. Insistence upon a political theory as the principle by which all educational policies are to be adjudicated is totalitarian radicalism.

Sentimentalism about the nature of the human being and this political fanaticism have thus combined to produce a concept of education treacherous to our regime. It represents the most overweening attempt of gnostic thinking to replace the natural structure of our society with their dream world, which is to substitute a subjective wishfulness for an historical reality.

From the beginning I have spoken of the progressive movement in education as an apostasy out of conviction that this classifies it accurately. An apostate is properly defined as one who, after making profession of a belief, falls away from or abandons it. So with the progressive educators. They profess before society a belief in education, and they are in fact supported by society for this profession. In reality, they are attackers and saboteurs of education. This truth I have tried to show by two lines of proof: namely, that the apostates do not have faith in the existence of knowledge, and that their real aim is the educationally illicit one of conditioning the young for political purposes. The fact that they do not believe in knowledge makes them manipulators or trainers rather than teachers, and this is the light in which we should understand their instrumentalist philosophy. The world for which the progressivists are conditioning their students is not the world espoused by general society, but by a rather small minority of radical doctrinaires and social faddists. They are doing things which the great majority of plain, uncorrupted individuals, from a standpoint in history and common sense, would repudiate if they could see their tendency.

This subversion has gone so far that gnostics of education until very recently constituted the greatest single threat to our culture. In the discredit that they have cast upon the higher faculties, in the way they have cut the young off from knowledge of the excellencies achieved in the past, and in the way they have turned attention toward transient externals and away from the central problem of man, they have no equal as an agency of subversion. Their schemes are exactly fitted, if indeed they are not designed, to produce citizens for the secular communist state, which is the millennial dream of the modern gnostic. To put an end to this adventure into fantasy and to prevent the cruel awakening which would follow, we should do all we can, educationally and politically, to hasten the decline of their influence.

EIGHT

The Reconsideration of Man

Not only the character but also the degree of a culture is responsive to the prevailing image of man. For what man tells himself he is manifests itself soon enough in what he does and may even predetermine what he can do. Historically speaking, man has been many things to himself, but the variation is only one side of the story. For if man has been many things, he is also one thing. Hovering over all the varieties is a harmonious ideal of man by which he must be judged if progression is to be at all possible. Even so empirical a thinker as John Stuart Mill, when he came to give his real or final reason justifying liberty, could not dispense with the imperative of this ideal. Now there are some images of man which impede this by holding people down to a low level of awareness and potentiality. The student of culture will be critical of all images that threaten true reaction—that is, reversion toward a poorer and less truthful concept of what it means to be a human being.

We must admit that man has been living with himself for many thousands of years without discovering completely what he is. But it is impossible to think that he has discovered nothing; that would be less credible than to suppose that he has discovered everything. I should think that if there is one thing that man has learned about himself, it is that he is a creature of choice. A corollary to this discovery is that he is a creature of dignity. His dignity arises from his power of choice; it comes from the very precariousness and peril of his position, so that his dignity is something that he has perpetually to maintain by exercise. It is these qualities which make him different from the social insects and leave him capable of creating rational cultures—rational in the sense that they express a relationship of human ends and means.

Now it must be further admitted that the development of man's self-knowledge has not been consistently forward. Rather, its history has been fraught with vicissitudes; there have been delays, back-trackings, even dark nights of the mind in which he seemed to know much less about himself than previous generations had done. The imminence of such a dark night of the mind is the subject of this essay.

One of the dilemmas of the modern world is that while the idea of the freedom and dignity of man is increasingly held up as the sanction of government and the goal of personal endeavor, other lines of reasoning, from other quarters, converge to make this belief seem untenable. Man is being told by the representatives of that body of knowledge which today enjoys the most prestige that he is not free, while it is being urged upon him by statesmen and leaders of opinion that freedom is the basis of his laws and institutions. At no other time in history have there been so many apostrophes to freedom and so much inner doubt as to whether the word stands for a reality. Two sources that the average person has been taught to respect come to him with opposite conclusions, and it is not to be wondered if his own conclusions become tentative and confused.

The conclusions which work toward undermining his idea of freedom come from science, although not always directly from the scientists. The dominant mood has been to accept what "science says" as an ipse dixit and then to see what, if anything, can be salvaged after its pronouncements have been conceded. It is my conviction that we do not have to fall back so far. We can offer defense and even attack at some of the outer works where the scientists deal with their own facts in their own way. In other words, we can show that some of the scientific claims are not scientifically based or are not rationally argued. Saving the image of man on which our culture depends requires that we make full use of these strategies.

We may well feel it curious that modern man has allowed himself to be pushed back so far in his efforts to defend his dignity and his freedom. I spoke a moment before of certain "lines of reasoning" which have had the effect of reducing him in his own eyes. They are such as far as their formal nature goes, but they are hardly valid reasonings. They are on the contrary illogical deductions from certain of the admitted facts of science. These have been used to remove man from a place "a little lower than the angels" to one where he is only the king of the beasts, and a king whose freedom is illusory. Yet it seems that the whole trend can be met and stopped by a little reflective reasoning on the reasoning processes themselves. I propose therefore to review certain steps in the progressive demotion of man. Let us begin then with what is referred to as his "dignity," remembering that "dignity" by derivation means "worth." Why is man worth less in his own eyes than he was in the eyes of his ancestors ten generations ago?

The first suspicious deduction concerning the status of man came by way of astronomy. Some three centuries ago it was discovered that the heavens do not revolve around our planet. Observation and theory since that time have revealed that the earth is a very small part of the universe which can be seen or assumed to exist. Not only is it very small in comparison with other aggregations of matter, but it is not even centrally located. It lies off in some odd corner, away from the "important" center.

These facts may be vivid, but what is their real implication? It is easy enough to trace what has been drawn from them. From the fact that the earth is very small in comparison with the rest of the matter in the universe and from the fact that its position is eccentric, it has been inferred that man has a very small significance in the totality.

But this is not the kind of thinking that passes muster with the logically trained mind or with any intelligent mind. Passing from the physical insignificance of the globe on which man dwells to his own insignificance commits the fallacy of sliding terms, since the term "insignificance" here changes meaning. The proponents of the argument cannot get from something that is measured quantitatively to something that is qualitative without an illicit process. The reasoning, let us note again, purports to show that because man's home is small, his importance must be small. The underlying assumption is that the Creator must have distributed his matter pro rata, with what is very important getting a great deal and what is less important getting less. But what is the standard of importance? We do not value animals so crudely; we do not say that because the elephant contains more matter in the form of protoplasm than the horse it is therefore a more valuable animal or one more favored by creation. There are no standards of valuation apart from the human or the divine. If one planet supports life and a whole galaxy supports none, there is nothing to give the galaxy a claim to greater significance. It is conceivable that the Creator made for man a small and somewhat out of the way pasture, but a very green one and one adequate to his needs. I cannot follow the reasoning which says that if man is to be considered important, he must inhabit one of the largest globes in space and that this must have a position at the center. Much of the universe might seem a waste of matter, but what is the meaning here of "waste"? The term seems to invoke the farmer's economy. "Waste" has no meaning where matter can be created out of nothing, and where, perhaps, there is delight in the act of creation. The inference drawn from location is whimsical.

Yet as it happened this enlarged view of the physical universe had the effect of reducing man proportionately in importance. Those who continued to speak of him as the cynosure of creation were ridiculed as illogical, but it seems to me that the illogic is mainly on the other side.

About the middle of the last century the second wave of depreciation came through the influence of Darwin's theory of the descent of man. The effect of this was to place man squarely in the animal kingdom. For the evolutionists stressed not man's distinctness, but his similarity to other animals. They traced his origin back hundreds of millions of years to the primeval slime, and although they acknowledged distinctive development through specialization, they taught that he was a member of the anthropoid tribe—"an ape reft of his tail and grown rusty at climbing," as James Branch Cabell wittily phrased it. They emphasized, moreover, that man had developed through the same pressures as the other animals and that the law of the survival of the biologically fittest applied to him no less than to the denizens of field and forest. A few left room for the supposition that at some point a divine spark might have entered into his composition, but their main story was of the progressive evolution of man out of a simpler and more primitive type of animal.

Man had already been deprived, as we have just seen, of his central position in the universe; now he lost hope that he was a unique kind of creation, on however small and insignificant a planet. The image he entertained of himself had to be narrowed down further. He was one of the animals and he could not be expected to behave differently from them—indeed, to behave differently might be to risk survival. If the story of man was but the story of an animal, was it really deserving of the sublime treatment it had been given in religion and literature? Many inferences adverse to social morality and even culture could be drawn. Some encouragement, it was suggested, might be found in the realization that man was now on his own and could fashion his future himself, although theories of determinism were to arise and undermine the latter supposition. Maybe the new enlightenment should have made him feel more responsible but it actually made him feel less so. More than likely what this revelation inspires in the average consciousness is the thought, "Well, if we are animals, let's be real ones."

I recognize that any layman's criticism of the theory of evolution will appear to most people today as reckless. The amount of study given the theory has been so extensive, the alleged proofs are from so many sources and are so massive in appearance, and the evolutionists have so much "liberal" opinion on their side that the average person who is still reluctant to accept its implications feels that he may as well shrug in hopelessness and say, "I surrender." Indeed the layman must not presume to question the facts assembled by qualified scientists (although what constitutes a fact is itself sometimes debatable). Nevertheless, we need to look at the matter from a greater perspective and remember that no science exists purely in the form of a collection of facts. The sciences are these facts plus structures of reasoning that are built upon them. The facts we are bound to receive if they come from sources that have given satisfactory evidence of their objectivity. But the reasoning that is done upon the basis of them is open to the inquiry of every man who has a rational faculty. Even in religious matters a certain amount of rational apprehension on the part of the communicant is indispensable—the meanings of certain propositions he is expected to understand and the meanings of imperatives he is supposed to carry out. It is certainly not less so with science: if men are to be convinced that they are simply the products of evolution, the convincing must be done in accordance with the necessary laws of thought. This is merely saying that the layman has the right to ask about the connection between the factual evidence and the conclusion when that connection is not apparent to him. He has the right to ask philosophical questions about the way the facts have been handled and even about whether all of the relevant facts have been taken into consideration.

On the permissibility of doing this, I wish to cite a distinguished biologist, Professor Edmund W. Sinnott of Yale, who has written the following:

> ... if the idealist will admit that *life* is his final problem and will halt his retreat to heights where the scientist is unable to follow him, he can successfully do battle at the level of biology itself and on its terms. Here he has the opportunity not only to defend himself but at last to counterattack the position of his adversary. In this combat let both opponents employ every scientific and dialectical force at their command to solve life's riddle, and agree to abide by the result. In that day when the verdict is finally rendered there will doubtless be surprises for both in store.[1]

Although I cannot hold Professor Sinnott responsible for inviting what I am going to say, I draw attention to his statement that the dialectical approach may have something to contribute to the final solution.

With this as prologue I list a few objections which seem to me to leave the evolutionary hypothesis somewhat less than overwhelmingly convincing.

First and most generally, the theory of evolution can be viewed as a form of the question-begging fallacy. It demands an initial acceptance of the doctrine of naturalism before any explanation is offered. Specifically, when the biologist is faced with the fact of the enormous differentiation and specialization in nature, he says that these were caused by the proximate method which nature would use, *assuming that nature is the only creative force that exists*. For example, it is admitted by biologists that complete empirical data for the descent of man from the lower animals is missing. The problem then becomes how to fit him into a scheme where nothing is allowed to appear except through natural causation. Thus it is reasoned that if man possesses the largest brain found in nature, it is because it must have been utilitarian for him to develop a large brain. But how can this be proved except by reference to the a priori postulate that nothing develops except through organic need? Again and again in the literature of evolution one finds that things are viewed as "necessary" because they come from this assumed natural cause rather than as proved because they come from a known cause. In other words the fact that things have come into being is used as evidence that nature must have used the evolutionary process to bring them into being. I submit that this reasoning does not prove evolution a fact: it rather assumes that evolution is a fact and then uses it as both cause and effect in describing the phenomena of nature. It is an ascertained truth that species do undergo change. But it is not in the spirit of free inquiry to hold the cause of that change down to a pattern of response between the organism and its environment in the interest of life. Here is where the theory slips in the questionable premise we have mentioned.

Even this account, however, is not without difficulties for the biologists. The pressure of environment alone seems not to explain the adaptation of organisms. There remains the task of accounting for the enormous variety of living things. How could simple environmental influence have called forth the giraffe, the centipede, the butterfly, the orchid, the sunflower? For this phase of the explanation the biologists bring in the theory of mutation. Mutations are chemical alterations in the genes which produce genetic variants which *may* permit a species to make a favorable adaptation to an environment. But two things at least seem to leave the theory of mutation wrapped in mystery. First, the scientists admit that they do not know how they occur. Second, species are found to contain mutants which are not related to their present needs for adaptation. In other words, mutations may occur long (and in the timetable of evolution "long" may mean a very long while) before there is any need for them to insure the survival of the species.[2] What this suggests is a kind of preadaptation, with the species being armed far in advance for some crisis it will meet in the future. The scientific explanation of this is that it is nature's method to throw out ever new possibilities, to provide a vast proliferation at the cost of staggering waste in the form of mutants which are not needed and species which do not make the grade in adjustment. Yet this seems to leave the whole matter inscrutable. It is not accurate, for example, to say that an environment of a certain kind will force a species to develop protective coloring, because some members will and some will not. Change is not, then, a simple predictable response of an organism to surroundings. We must now rely upon nature's illimitable fertility in preadaptation to explain how some things get through. It was "provided" that the way should be left for some things to survive. But this is the kind of providence that might suggest to our total awareness an inscrutable purpose.

At the very least, the invoking of mutation disposes of mechanical causation and leaves the biologist to bridge the gap with some concept of emergence. The idea of an emergent is itself a concealed assumption, since it involves a place where the causal link is not known but is supposed to exist anyhow. The empirical data are neither complete nor rigorous enough to exclude the possibility of some kind of intervention or preintervention.

Moreover the theory of natural selection is not without its problems. One of the most puzzling of these concerns is the early stage of an adaptive organ. It is easy enough to perceive the usefulness of an organ like the fully developed wing or eye. But of what use was this when it first began to develop, when it was rudimentary and perhaps microscopically small? Could its usefulness then have been decisive enough to make the difference between survival and extinction? Given the broad nature of the forces that living organisms are up against, would these early tiny modifications spell the difference between life and death? The evolutionists answer this by emphasizing the slowness of evolution. Only let the period be long enough, they say, and these improbabilities will issue in present actualities. On one occasion Darwin himself was queried regarding this objection. He returned the answer that such a process of development might be inconceivable to the imagination but it is not so to the reason. Yet I am left wondering whether this is an effective answer. It is perhaps conceivable to the reason if we accept certain lines of causality and exclude others and adjust the time interval accordingly. But imagination may have something to introduce which would make the development less dependent on time and infinitesimal change.

When we turn to the special subject of the evolution of man, other difficulties manifest themselves. The most insuperable of these is the mystery of the origin of language. Students approaching this through the route of anthropology have about given up the problem as hopeless. The best attempts to explain the origin of speech naturalistically rest upon feeble analogies. There is no anthropological or naturalistic account which is any more convincing than the mythological one that speech was a gift to man. What we do know is that language is specifically human in occurrence, that is, it is a specifically human endowment. Animals communicate among themselves by signs but a sign is a different thing from a verbal symbol. A sign is something imitative of or closely connected with what it indicates, as may be seen when we use the hand to beckon or the finger to point.

What we more than suspect is that all language is metaphorical in its origin, and the use of metaphor is distinctively intellectual and non-naturalistic, because metaphor disengages the word from the thing. At the same time it sets up a new level of meaning which relates the word to the thing and to something else. Here emerges the wider consciousness of meaning and the whole rich storehouse of transferred significations. A metaphor implies the world of symbolism, which is a world of transcendence over the merely natural. We cannot say whether man came into possession of this world gradually or suddenly or whether he had full access to it from his "creation," because the history of this attainment is veiled from us. But it is a datum which has to be accounted for. The most one can do now is fall back upon the idea of emergence that supposes there was a cause which somehow induced man to make the kind of effort that issues in language. But again one feels that he is being asked to make concessions to preserve the integrity of a theory. It seems better to say that we are here confronted with a mystery which makes man if not a special creation as the religionists have said, at least the possessor of very special capacities.

In net estimate the theory of organic evolution as applied to man is a partial philosophy of man's place in the universe. It has evidently been promulgated with a strong anterior desire to submit man to nature. Yet there have been in the past more comprehensive philosophic views which visualized man in nature without leaving him blindly immersed in it or subject only to a single cause. When Immanuel Kant was a young man, he accepted in his *The General Theory of Nature and Theory of the Heavens* a thoroughgoing mechanism in the realm of all nature; but much later, when he came to write his *The Teleological Faculty of Judgment*, he took a more conservative view. In the latter he found it necessary to invoke teleology for the organic realm. Kant was willing to concede the development of species out of one common original parent, but he could not accept the idea of blind purpose: ". . . the archeologist of Nature . . . must for this end ascribe to the common mother, an organization ordained purposely with a view to the needs of all her offspring; otherwise the possibility of suitability of form in the products of the animal and vegetable kingdoms cannot be conceived at all."[3] Long before this Aristotle had held that each form in nature had a formal cause, "an inner perfecting tendency," which worked to preserve the unity of type. This theory, says Professor Henry Fairfield Osborn, left Aristotle halfway between physics and metaphysics. I suggest that this is where the idealist, believing in the specialty of the human being, while embracing all the knowledge of man and of nature which has accumulated since that time, will choose to stand. The formulations above are not offered as final. The need now is for some genius of thought who will bring all these concepts together and show how that unique condition of entropy which is man owes its existence to something more than a blind swirl of protoplasm. The final solution must accommodate the ideas lying behind our feeling that the appearance of man on earth was a destined miracle.

I have tried to sketch some grounds on which the student
of man may enter a demurrer without losing entirely his intellectual responsibility. Yet we must recognize that the notoriety,
if not the reasoning, of the evolutionists' case has caused it to
be very widely accepted that man is one of the animals, with
like origin, like behavior, and like extinction. This has effected
a second major change in man's evaluation of himself, and in
doing so it has further decreased his availability for roles that
require transcendental significance. We hear smooth words to
the effect that there is no real conflict between science and
religion or between science and literature. There is no real conflict anywhere when one side gives up. The question still at issue
is whether the facts and the logic dictate so complete a surrender as has been urged on one party.

Once the aggressions of science had man comfortably en-
sconced in nature in this manner, the next step was at hand.
This was to immerse him entirely in material causality. If his
being and shape were due to natural laws, which could be stud-
ied as phenomena, why not account for the whole of him, including his famous free will, in the same way? In this fashion
materialistic determinism followed hard upon Darwinism.
Scientific study had shown the law of causality operating in
areas where previously miracles and mysteries were thought to
occur, and this was a mandate for science to continue its study
until the last phenomenon had been explained in an equally
scientific way. The law of physical causality was therefore pos-
ited as general, and it was assumed that these phases of human
conduct which are now unexplainable are so because there has

not been sufficient investigation to determine all the factors. When science has attained its goal, it will be possible, so the supposition has gone, to predict the behavior of the individual human being or of the political group to which he belongs, in the same way as it is possible to predict that rabbits will eat lettuce.

This bold claim encounters serious objections when submitted to the laws of evidence. The verdict "Not Proven" must be entered unless it can be shown either that man has no such thing as a spirit, being a material automaton only; or that if he does have a spirit, it is not merely influenced but is completely dominated by the material factors making up his body. Now the "proof that man does not have a spirit cannot be said to rest on anything more than asseveration. It is the consensus of the great body of mankind—civilized, semicivilized, and uncivilized—that he does have. The feeling rests upon a kind of immediate apprehension that there is something more to man than the body he carries around. It is connected with the feeling most of us experience that the body and the spirit do sometimes conflict. The body has some relation with the spirit; it provides it with a home during this phase of its existence and charges it room and board, as Eliseo Vivas has put it. But there are times when the spirit seems to rise up in its God-given sovereignty and tell the body to go too. There is more empirical evidence for this belief than for the contrary one. All that those who urge this materialism have is a series of deductions from "laws" which are not themselves unassailable. If the universe is such and such, and if man is such and such, then he does not have one. But this proof looks thin compared with the assurance given by our consciousness. Increasingly the scientists are asking us to believe things that are contrary to the witness of our senses, and what is possibly more serious, contrary to the testimony of our intuitions. It is now with reference to *their* teachings that the poor layman has to say, "I believe, help thou mine unbelief."

Recently, however, those who argue that man is not free because he is part of the universe of matter have met difficulties on more scientific ground. For example, a good many social scientists have supposed that the statistical method would give us the key to human behavior. Only let enough data be collected, and let the data be run through computing machines, and have on hand a staff of scientists to draw the conclusions, and the random element in human conduct would no longer trouble us. The collected and analyzed data would tell us for certain whether a designated individual would become a leading citizen in the community, or would turn criminal, or would commit suicide, or would develop an "authoritarian" personality, or whatever else. These expectations have proved wrong. The most that this kind of counting and analysis can establish is a statistical probability regarding the group as a whole. That is to say, we may arrive at a statistical probability that a certain number of persons out of one million will commit suicide in the course of a year. Yet this gives us no basis for predicting that one John Smith, living at a certain address, will be a suicide. There is no way of prefiguring his response to his environment by reference to such averages.

Finally, it is now being suspected by the physicists—the advanced guard of modern science—that the behavior of matter is itself finally unpredictable. It is even suggested that indeterminacy may be an ultimate characteristic of matter. This seems a break of crucial importance in the front of rigid physical and mechanical causation. If the new theory is true, it forestalls the effort of those who have been trying to drive man into a trap by progressively reducing him to physical bases. For if the ultimate constituents of matter are unpredictable in their behavior, where along the line is one going to establish the principle of determinacy? And of course if man is something more than matter, then the argument against determinacy for him becomes a fortiori.

We have now noted how man has been cut down in his own sight in three ways. He has been told of his cosmic insignificance; he has been informed that he must class himself as an animal, and he has been left in doubt as to whether he is a free agent. These assertions, made with increasing boldness over the present span of time, have rather thoroughly percolated the public mind and have produced an attitude forbidding to his religious and poetic representation. That they have had a baneful influence upon culture can be shown, I think, by appealing to the broad history of literature, which I choose as one of the most various and complete expressions of man's spirit.

What I shall relate is not so much a story of progressive degeneration as it is a story of successive retreats before the growing "scientific" image of man. It is a noteworthy fact that high tragedy began to disappear from the literature of our

Western culture at the end of the seventeenth century, which was the very time that science first staked out its great claims. These claims seem to have undermined rather suddenly the kind of vision that leads the gifted creator to produce great pictures of man's tragic situation. In order to appreciate a tragic representation, one has to believe first of all that man is important—to himself and to whatever transcendental powers may be. One has to believe also that he has a freedom of moral choice curiously related to a fatal ignorance. This means that while gaining insights into reality, one has to reconcile oneself to the ultimate perplexity and mysteriousness of this life. Such ideas are not compatible with the dogma of infinite progress or the belief that man's dominion is potentially unlimited. Tragedy presents a universe still unknowable when it depicts man as incapable of learning enough in time to insure his happiness. Science as the great unraveler of mystery promised to end this situation, and its growing influence seems thus related to the decline of tragedy.

Man still had enough human ground to stand on for satire, however, and the following century was the great age of satire. This may be understood as the first defensive position after tragedy has been yielded up. Satire is highly human just because it is critical. By the nature of his art, the satirist maintains a position of superiority to his subjects. From this position he wields a lash upon man for his follies and aberrations. In satire description is not validation; description is condemnation, and the satirist is judge. This cannot fail to mean that the satirist envisages a proper role and destiny for man. He sees man as human in the sense of bearing obligations, and his real subject is human delinquency. Satire does not indeed contain the *dianoia* of tragedy, but it does recognize good and evil and the principle of responsibility. It focuses upon man in a world of values, and it requires an espousal of values by an audience to appreciate the literature of satire. By the eighteenth century, people had been forced out of one position, but they had room enough left to make possible a great satirical literature. The difference between Shakespeare on the one hand and Swift and Pope on the other is wide, but Swift and Pope present a literary treatment of man.

By the nineteenth century the awareness of science was much greater, and satire, with its human evaluation, disappeared. This is, of course, a mixed period, which offers obstacles to generalization. One outstanding development, however, was the flowering of the novel.[4] The novel is the loosest of the literary forms, and perhaps this is a sign that the age was trying to do something, if only partly consciously, about the restrictions that were crowding in. Perhaps it was an attempt to say that if man cannot have tragic grandeur or moral status, he can at least have history. Novels are in a way histories of their characters, and some have been entitled histories. One notes at the same time a rather steady turning toward realism and naturalism—that is, to the depiction of man as he is outwardly and visibly, and to man as a creature of circumstance, which is a parallel to the scientific treatment of him. With a few outstanding exceptions, the belief that the critical field of battle is the moral consciousness fades out.

The twentieth century is so near at hand and so variegated that it is perhaps even more difficult to generalize about. There is some indication that the novel has reached a dead end and is ceasing to be a vital literary form. While large numbers continue to be published, they are increasingly chronicles of the abnormal, the aberrant, and even the criminal; they present their characters as products of material psychological conditioning, with narrow horizons of consciousness. When writers like William Faulkner and Robert Penn Warren do present in fiction the human dilemma, their works are often not read for what they are. The public, and in many cases the critics, seize upon some incidental aspect of them and interpret this as reflecting "today's thinking." The pressure against reporting the whole man in a moral situation has indeed not silenced such writers, but it has left them widely misunderstood.

It is true that nondramatic poetry has had a brilliant revival, although there is ground for fearing that this depends too much upon psychological intensity and experimental daring. Literary criticism has attained a volume and developed a complexity beyond anything seen before. This too is a brilliant achievement, but it has been suggested by more than one thoughtful source that such preoccupation with criticism is a sign of exhaustion of the creative impulse. Criticism is the looking over and the assessment of what has been done in creative hours, which are hours of warm blood and of feeling. Is this criticism an attempt to save literature by proving explicitly what literature itself ought to be left to show implicitly? Many persons are unhappy over the critical predominance, and few seem to feel that it is a prelude to a renascence of that wonder out of which literature as well as philosophy has always sprung.

These are a few of the empirical evidences that the erroneously adduced scientific image of man is steadily taking away the room in which literature has flourished. I admit that it is difficult to prove a conclusion by these means, because pieces of empirical evidence look different and carry different weight in the eyes of different observers. In any case, they cannot be estimated without reference to underlying principles. Let us therefore go back to the essentials of the problem and ask what literature could do with the new man which the scientists and their attaches are ushering upon the stage.

All literature depends upon belief that part of man, or man in his essential definition, is unconditioned; and in consequence, the end of literature is portended when the contrary idea, that man is wholly conditioned, takes hold. When we think about the nature of tragedy, we recognize that every tragic story is about a being who potentially is, and actually should be, discerning and free, but who gets entangled in something which "conditions" him to the extent of obscuring his discernment and ending his freedom. The tragic struggle itself is between this spiritual and unconditioned man and the forces that conspire against that conditionless state. The man comes upon the scene free, happy, and confident, enjoying a career of prosperity. He enters into a situation where, in comparison with his previous ones, he is ignorant. This is where his ignorance, or a bent of character which obscures his judgment, begins to preponderate and set him on the downward path. The tragic flaw is always this susceptibility to losing one's freedom of choice where right choice is necessary to salvation. Our response to the tragic depends upon a belief that some men become in this sense conditioned and others do not. But in the world of the scientific outlook which we have just surveyed, all men are equally conditioned and hence all careers are equally tragic or untragic. Now if in spite of this we believe in the reality of tragedy, we value the literary expression of it because that teaches us to beware of—or, as some would be content with saying, apprises us of—the danger of that kind of conditioning. The whole tradition of tragedy is thus seen to be antiscientific. Tragedy is a lament that man should ever lose his unconditional freedom to cope with circumstances.

A similar set of factors explains comedy, for the comic character is conditioned or imprisoned although with less painful result. We see him as a man like ourselves, made to be free but in a situation where he is not free. He may be dominated by some weakness, as in the old comedy of humors, or, as in some of the modern sadistic cartoons, he may be tossed and blown about by forces too great for him to withstand. He may be a character who is accustomed to one milieu, where he moves freely; but now he is in a different one, and everything he does is awkward because he does not understand. This is why Henri Bergson maintains in his treatise on the comic that comic effect always involves the temporary suspension of the individual's free will. If the dignified man in the top hat steps on a banana peel and slips to the ground, we laugh, because we know that is the very thing he would *not* do if he had full command of himself. For a few brief seconds he has been wholly at the disposition of physical forces. That is the condition the true man is never found in, and hence our feeling that it is comical. But it would not be comical if we did not have in mind the contrast between man as a free agent and the funny man who is the antithesis of this idea. Yet no strict materialist could laugh at the spectacle of the dignified gentleman slipping to the ground. According to his system, this is the one condition in which men are always and invariably; they are being pushed, pulled, or thrown around by the larger world of which they are a part. Their roles in the action are not responses but reactions, in the physical sense of that term. If human consciousness and will do not enter into the series of causes, there is nothing to sympathize with or to laugh at; there is only the passage of impulse from one thing to another. All effort to dignify man requires that we see him as experiencing something more than eventualities.

Thus the existence of literature depends on our willingness to take a *serious* view of man. In his *Language as Gesture*, R. P. Blackmur has written that "it takes a strong and active prejudice to see facts at all," and to this he adds that "the sensibility must have a pretty firm anterior conviction about the nature of poetry in order to wake up to a given body of poetry at all."[5] Broadening this somewhat, I would say that it takes a strong and original feeling about man to see some of the things he does and is capable of doing. Without this original prejudice, which I employ here in the sense of a conception, one cannot regard man as worthy of the literary kind of depiction.

No person in the practice of living really thinks of himself as a simple aggregate of the calcium, iron, phosphorus, and other elements to which he is reducible chemically. He thinks of himself as a creation consisting of more than the sum of all of these and as a being having the power of self-conduct. This is the kind of image that traditional man, out of his intuitions and human preferences, constructed of himself. He felt that just as there was a special danger, so there was a special glory in his being "chosen." For he was "not of the common kind," the common kind being the nonrational and nonspiritual forms of life. With such a representation before him, he could look to Sophocles, Dante, and Shakespeare for his justification.

There never occurred to the pre-science ancients, to make the point clearer, a doubt that the proper study of mankind is man. That it is, is the premise of all classical literature, and this is the fountain from which the great tradition of humanism flows down to our time. Always the subject of classical literature was the human being, what he was doing in the world, and what his responsibility was when his eyes were lifted up to the horizon. Underlying any such premise is a feeling which can be identified only with affection. No one writes creatively and continuously about something which he dislikes. It has been justly observed that creative artists love even their villains. To write about man in the literary way is certainly not to prove that "one loves one's fellow man" in the sentimental and banal sense, but that one does separate him out from other beings and regards his destiny as something no member of human kind should be indifferent to. Neither is it to affirm that man is

"good" in the sentimental and romantic sense. Rather, it is to
affirm that man is a critical problem. "The glory, jest, and riddle
of the world," a great poet has termed him.[6]

Now while man has many times claimed goodness arising
from a divine connection and while he is given to erecting
codes of ethics, he has committed the most abominable crimes
and has visited every kind of suffering upon his fellows for an
infinite variety of alleged reasons. He is passionate and unsta-
ble, so that very little is required to set him on the warpath, even
against his kith and kin. Most fearful of all to contemplate is
his great power of self-deception. He often does things for reasons that are obscure to him, and undoubtedly many a person
has led an entire life in ignorance of the mainspring of his own
actions.

These things being so, nothing could be more proper to
man than the study of himself, and it is important that this
should be the deepest, freest, and most imaginative that the
most gifted individuals are capable of making. It should be a
continuing, earnest examination of human life, with all its
moods, impulses, choices of means, failures and successes, mis-
eries and happinesses shown in concrete representation. The
indispensable requirement, both for the creation and the enjoyment of literature thus conceived, is a receptivity to the real
image of man. The practical problem is how to restore that
receptivity in the face of a barbarism nourished by the scientistic fallacies discussed earlier.

A simple illustration may make this clearer. Every teacher
of experience knows that there is a type of student who resents

the very idea of studying literature. This student hangs back or is even defiant because he senses that the study of literature demands a certain kind of intellectual and emotional response. We might say that it demands a sign of consent, almost like some religious sacraments. It requires of every man that he suppress at least part of his native barbarism and enter into rapport with the realm of value. The easier and more natural thing for him to do is to regard the work of literature with mingled contempt and truculence. For literature, at the same time it pleases those who accept it, imposes obligations; one does not enter into it and leave scot-free. In that important respect literature is further comparable to religion; it is not supposed to make us merely comfortable. This the wary barbarian (even in the form of the reluctant student) senses, and he may decide to persist in an obdurate barbarism. It is part of the barbarian's self-protection to reject cultivation. He may repel all influences that would mollify the attitude that keeps him narrow and destructive. Putting this in a figurative way, one might assert that men are not ready for literature until they have been "Christianized." By this I refer to the establishment of that "prejudice" Blackmur speaks of in *Language as Gesture*. They must give initial assent to certain propositions about man and the world. In no age are all men equally ready to give this assent, and in our age there are new active forces to persuade them against giving it. The barbarian's picture of the world is founded upon simple adulation of force, direct ways of satisfying appetite, and generally the absence of any idea about human destiny. (Of course not all peoples who have been called barbarians fit this description.) When the barbarian is asked to respect things which rebuke, refine, and control these ideas, he is being asked to change his way of life. Hence the problem of conversion arises, which in the modern setting will have to be away from the idealization of physical comfort, from the view of life as the mere play of physical matter, and from the short-cutting of those processes around which cultured man weaves patterns of significance. It must be a conversion to an awareness of the ethical and religious drama of every moment.

The last observation introduces a final phase of the problem. If we should agree that literature is now beset with forces which mean its eventual extinction, are we faced with loss of an irreparable kind? I feel that an affirmative answer to this has already been given in substance, but let me summarize here my reasons for saying that literature cannot be spared if culture of the highest form is to endure. Literature is the keystone of the arch of culture. Not only is it the most various, searching, and "complete" of the forms, but it is the form in which an intellectual culture stores the ideas from which a society derives its rhetoric of cohesion and impulsion. If this goes, we cannot be sure how much else will be allowed to remain, and the degeneration of culture is the road back to brutishness.

It should be more widely appreciated that culture is an intermediary between man and his highest vocation, which in some form or other is a matter of the spirit. But it is not the nature of the mass of men to be spiritual at every moment in the saint's way. Part of their devoir they can pay through due observance of and due tribute to the forms of their culture.

These, in their various manifestations, are daily reminders that men are something more than eating, defecating, and mating animals. There is always in cultural observance a little gesture of piety, a recognition that there are higher demands on man along with the lower. While culture is not a worship and should not be made a worship, it is a kind of orienting of the mind toward a mood, a reverence for the spirit on secular occasions. Then there is the further consideration that a culture is a protection against fanaticism both of the political and the religious kinds. If there is nothing but a vacancy between men and their political or religious ideal, the response to this may be without the rationality and grace of measure. But if these ideals are expressed in a thousand kindly and attractive forms in the creations of a culture, mere fierceness is mollified and the manner and approach are made right. Thus art and manners are seen to have a relation to politics and religion, not teaching them in any simple or direct sense, but providing a bridge by which one is helped to pass from one kind of cognition to another. This is the highest reason of all for desiring to preserve the basis of our culture, which we have now seen to be threatened by pseudo-scientific images of man.

NOTES

Preface

1. Letter from Richard Weaver to Richard Cornuelle dated Thanksgiving Day, 1954, acquired from the estate of Mrs. Polly Weaver Beaton. In addition to the specific items quoted, this discussion has been informed by documents in the collected papers of Cleanth Brooks (housed at Yale University), Donald Davidson (at Vanderbilt University), William C. Mullendore (at the University of Oregon), and Henry Regnery (at the Hoover Institution), documents in the files of the Louisiana State University Press, the Intercollegiate Studies Institute and *Modern Age*, and correspondence provided by Louis H. T. Dehmlow, the late Russell Kirk, and the family of Frank S. Meyer.

2. The full text of *Visions of Order* was also reprinted in the Conservative Book Club's *Omnibus Volume 6*, published in 1966.

3. Eliseo Vivas, "The Mind of Richard Weaver," *Modern Age* (Summer 1964), 307.

4. Letter from Richard M. Weaver to Kenneth S. Templeton dated October 16, 1957, in the Richard Malcolm Weaver Papers at Vanderbilt University. Quoted by permission.

5. Letter from Richard M. Weaver to Kenneth S. Templeton dated August 30, 1960, acquired from the estate of Mrs. Polly Weaver Beaton.

6. Ibid.

7. The friend was Eugene Davidson, editor of *Modern Age*, who commented on Chapter 6, "A Dialectic on Total War." He recommended only minor revisions.

8. See the letter from Richard M. Weaver to Dean Terrill dated September 3, 1960, in the Richard M. Weaver Library Collection at Hillsdale College.

9. See, for example, Eugene D. Genovese, *The Southern Tradition* (Cambridge, MA, 1994), and Bernard K. Duffy and Martin Jacobi, *The Politics of Rhetoric: Richard M. Weaver and the Conservative Tradition* (Westport, CT, 1993).

10. See, especially, Kirk's *America's British Culture* (New Brunswick, NJ, 1993), which can almost be read as a companion volume to *Visions of Order*.

One

1. T. S. Eliot, *Notes Toward the Definition of Culture* (New York, 1949), 17.

2. An example of this is often seen in the relation of the academic person to the culture in which he lives. He may be and often is learned in it, but he is not exactly of it. I have felt more than once that this fact is proved by the peculiar explicitness of the speech of college professors. They are usually at great pains to draw out the meaning of their phrases and to verbalize all the connections of thought. Some of this may result from the habit of simplifying things for youthful learners, but this is not the whole account of it. In the speech of a culture maintained by a traditional society, there will occur many elisions and ellipses of meaning. It is not necessary to state them, because anyone can supply the omissions; it is rather the awkwardness of pedantry to put them into words. But the man who is outside the tradition, or who is self-consciously halfway between the tradition and something else, goes about it in a different way: its beliefs, values, and institutions are "objects" to him, and he refers to them with something of the objective completeness of the technical description. This is why professors "sound so funny" when they talk of something that is an everyday subject to the ordinary man. This ordinary man wonders why the professor, instead of using lumbering phrases to designate the obvious, cannot assume more. It may also explain why

professors as a class are suspected of dissidence. Their speech does not sound like the speech of a person who is perfectly solid with his tradition, which is oftentimes the case.

3. Lancelot Law Whyte, *The Next Development in Man* (New York, 1948), 188.

4. José Ortega y Gasset, "Morbid Democracy," *Modern Age: A Conservative Review* (Summer, 1957), 54.

5. Goethe, *Poetry and Truth From My Life* (2 vols.; London, 1913), II, 240.

6. Ibid., II, 241.

Two

1. It is now being pointed out that some of the new machines, especially those designed for armed combat, make such demands of rapid response and endurance that they can be operated only by those at their physical peak, which period lasts but a few years. To the extent that such individuals enjoy prestige and exercise leadership by virtue of this physical capacity, they will make the physical basis of life still more influential upon social and cultural ordering. This is another example of how man's technological creations are forcing him, even if good sense and preference stand in the way, into patterns of behavior and organization dictated by physical laws.

2. In a eulogy pronounced at the funeral of Robert Y. Hayne, George M. Duffie declared that in Charleston "high talents directed toward virtuous ends are never permitted to remain long without their appropriate reward." Such spirit had contributed to the making of this elegant capital, but it was beginning to languish before the spirit of caste. The emergence of caste had a stultifying effect also upon literary and intellectual activity. While Charleston preserved its respect for enterprise and its institution of recruitment, it was a creative center. But respect for intellect and for literary accomplishment declined in the face of a rising regard for status. On this subject, one may consult the letters of William Gilmore Simms, one of the most devoted and disillusioned of Charlestonians. The "Sahara of the Bozart" which H. L. Mencken was to attack so scathingly at the same time that he held up for admiration the virtues of the early

Southerners resulted from this general victory of status throughout the whole of the South.

3. Carl Bridenbaugh, *Myths and Realities: Societies of the Colonial South* (Baton Rouge, 1952), 117.

4. Elijah Jordan, *Business Be Damned* (New York, 1952), 17.

Three

1. Frederick Whilhelmsen, "History, Toynbee, and the Modern Mind: Betrayal of the West," *Modern Age* (Summer, 1957), 38.

2. Robert S. Woodworth, *Psychology* (New York, 1940), 349.

3. It is of remarkable interest here to find that Ralph Waldo Emerson, who did so much to pave the way for modern religious and social attitudes, was charged with this lack of conscience by his shrewdest critic, Henry James, Sr. Emerson, James wrote, "had no conscience . . . and lived by perception, which is an altogether lower or less spiritual faculty." Conscience, he explains, "was always intended as a rebuke and never as an exhilaration to the private citizen," and therefore Emerson was "all his days an arch traitor to our existing civilized regimen, inasmuch as he unconsciously set aside its fundamental principle in doing without conscience." Consequently, "he had apparently no private personality." See "Emerson," in *The Literary Remains of the Late Henry James* (Boston, 1885), 293–302. Emerson, a great prophet of the soul, was thus according to James fundamentally soulless, but he has been an influential source of proto-modern thinking about man's nature and responsibility.

4. William McDougall, *The Energies of Men* (New York, 1933), 54.

Four

1. Mortimer Adler, *Dialectic* (New York, 1927), 31.

2. *The Birth of Tragedy*, trans. Clifton Fadiman, Volume V in *The Philosophy of Nietzsche* (Modern Library Edition; 5 vols.; New York, 1937), 253.

3. Henry Cary (trans.), *The Apology*, Volume I in *The Works of Plato* (6 vols.; London, 1858).

4. *Rhetoric*, trans. Lane Cooper (London, 1932), 1355a.

5. This is also the point of the great tragedies written before Euripides, who, significantly, was the only tragedian that Socrates admired.

Five

1. René Guerdan, *Byzantium: Its Triumphs and Tragedy* (New York, 1956), 36.
2. It would be difficult to find a better illustration of this than the *Breviloquium* of St. Bonaventura (written *ca.* 1250). This is an exposition of Christian doctrine rationalized and formalized to the highest degree. Its very organization is arranged to exhibit the classical aesthetic properties of order, harmony, balance, and proportion. Facts are always given in unitary groups of three, four, and seven, significant numbers in Christian numerology; reasons are presented in the same groupings. The whole of Christian theology has been reduced to a perfect *form.* The dominant effect that emerges is an aesthetic one, such as proceeds from a complex but impeccable order.
3. The author recalls hearing an automobile salesman say to a customer, "You are going to fall in love with that car."
4. The attitude of these false formalists toward the human can be seen in the way that city people often condemn and insult country people. Urban living is always more formalized than rural living, and generally the larger the city, the more formalized it is. The people of the city begin to believe that these forms are respectable in and for themselves, and they lack understanding and sympathy for the human being who has never had to accommodate himself to them. They are not for him because they are not responses to his situation. Yet the city dweller is prone to think automatically that everyone should know them and reverence them. So far does this go that in Megalopolis the average inhabitant may be simply milked dry, or crushed under the weight of them, until his comparative lack of humanity becomes proverbial.

Six

1. Hans Jonas, "The Practical Uses of Theory," *Social Research,* XXVI (Summer, 1959), 141.

2. Ibid.

3. Arthur Ekirch, *The Decline of American Liberalism* (New York, 1955), 35.

4. Clifford Dowdey, *The Land They Fought For* (New York, 1955), 164.

5. See Warren P. Hassler, Jr., *General George B. McClellan, Shield of the Union* (Baton Rouge, 1956), 317–22.

6. See Moritz Busch, *Bismarck: Some Secret Pages of His History* (2 vols.; New York, 1898), I, 128.

7. At this point I shall anticipate an objection which might be made by referring to the history of ancient Greece. No one thinks of denying that the Greeks created one of the most brilliant cultures and civilizations in history. But anyone reading Thucydides will look in vain for much exhibition of chivalry in the treatment of prisoners and noncombatants, many of the former being slain outright, and many of the latter sold into slavery or exiled. In reply to this objection I would make a series of points. In the first place, the Greeks were a pre-Christian civilization, and I have given in the chapter "The Cultural Role of Rhetoric" reasons for believing that Christianity made a cultural and ethical contribution surpassing even the high-water mark of the Greeks. In the second place, the Greeks did acknowledge certain responsibilities toward their deities (such as the right of asylum in temples) which exerted some restraint upon their acts of violence even in war. These provided on occasion a kind of sanction embracing both sides. The restraints were not always respected, but they were there, and they were rather frequently invoked. In the third place, there is evidence that Greek thought was tending in the direction I have been defending. For example, Thucydides in commenting on the revolution in Corcyra has this to say (Book III, chap. 84): "Indeed men too often take upon themselves in the prosecution of their revenge to set the example of doing away with those general laws to which all alike can look for salvation in adversity, instead of allowing them to subsist against the day of danger when their aid may be required." Finally one needs to consider the fact, generally admitted by historians, that the Peloponnesian War marked the beginning of the decline of Greek civilization.

8. Kenneth Burke, *A Rhetoric of Motives* (New York, 1950), 332.

Seven

1. The theme of this chapter was suggested by Eric Voegelin's *The New Science of Politics* (Chicago, 1952).
2. *The Five Books of Tertullian Against Marcion,* trans. Peter Holmes (Edinburgh, 1868), 26.
3. Plotinus, *Enneads* (London: Faber and Faber, n.d.), 151.
4. F. C. Burkitt, *Church and Gnosis* (Cambridge, 1932), 43–44.
5. Ibid., 63–64.
6. Eliseo Vinas, *The Moral Life and the Ethical Life* (Chicago, 1950), 135.
7. A related fact which cannot be overlooked is that a public school system supported by tax money was a New England conception. Tracing back to a statute enacted in Massachusetts in 1647, this system spread through the other New England colonies and states and later over the country as a whole, although it was resisted by most of the Southern states until after the Civil War. Thus at the very time that these latter-day gnostics were coming to dominate New England thinking, the New England school system was being imitated by one state after another, including finally the Southern states. That it would serve as a pipeline for the gnostic philosophy of the leaders of New England opinion was virtually inevitable.
8. John Dewey, *The School and Society* (Chicago, 1943), 27.
9. John Dewey, *Schools of Tomorrow* (New York, 1915), 134.
10. Ibid., 117.
11. A striking illustration of this truth came to my attention some years ago. A young engineer, an ordinary member of his profession, with an indifference toward the fine arts, obtained a job with a radio broadcasting station. This station put half an hour of classical music on the air every day, and this young man had the duty of controlling volume. Naturally he had to listen very carefully in order to maintain this at a uniform level. This very circumstance of having to listen carefully to classical music in discharge of his duty caused him to hear in it things he had been unaware of, with the result that he became a devotee. If this accidental outside pressure had not forced him to give careful attention to these programs, he probably never would have been recruited into the ranks of music appreciators.

12.   See for example Joan Dunn, *Retreat from Learning: Why Teachers Can't Teach* (New York, 1955).

Eight

1.   Edmund W. Sinnott, *From Cell to Psyche* (Chapel Hill, 1950), 107.
2.   See Theodosius Dobzhansky, "On Methods of Evolutionary Biology and Anthropology," *American Scientist*, XLV (Dec, 1957), 386–87.
3.   Quoted in Henry Fairfield Osborn, *From the Greeks to Darwin* (New York, 1908), 99.
4.   The novel began in the eighteenth century, but these cultural phrases will be found to dovetail into one another.
5.   R. P. Blackmur, *Language as Gesture* (New York, 1952), 26.
6.   Alexander Pope, *Essay on Man*, ed. Maynard Mack (London, 1950), Epistle II, line 18.